LARRY GOSSELIN, OFM
Illustrated by Steve Kalar

Unshadowed Light

Poems inspired by
St. Clare of Assisi

Unshadowed Light

Poems Inspired by St. Clare of Assisi
Larry Gosselin, OFM

Cover and inside illustrattions: Steve Kalar
Photography: Mary Kay Fry
Editor: Miki Landseadel
Cover and book design: Tau Publishing Design Department

For information regarding permission, write to:
Tau Publishing, LLC
Attention: Permissions Dept.
4727 North 12th Street
Phoenix, AZ 85014

ISBN 978-1-61956-261-5

First Edition April 2015
10 9 8 7 6 5 4 3 2 1

Published and printed in the United States of America by Tau Publishing, LLC.

♲ Text printed on 30% post-consumer waste recycled paper.

For additional inspirational books visit us at TauPublishing.com

TauPublishing.com
Words of Inspiration

Beauty is what fills the pages of this book! From the design and form of the poetry to the luminous illustrations that accompany Fr. Larry's prayer and poetic reflection, this collection is bound to invite readers to slow down, contemplate, and see the world anew with the "unshadowed light" that is the Spirit's illumination of all God's beautiful creation.

Daniel P. Horan, OFM,
Author of *Francis of Assisi and the Future of Faith* (2012)
and *The Franciscan Heart of Thomas Merton* (2014)

In the beautiful collection of poetry and art, Fr. Larry Gosselin discloses an inner light that penetrates the hidden corners of fragile humanity. Taking Clare of Assisi as his luminary guide, Fr. Gosselin travels the winding road of the spirit's journey into God. His poems are brief snapshots of what lies within when we can let go of everything that gets in the way of God and let in the bright rays of divine love. This is a book that can be read over and over because it chock full of treasured insights that speak to the timeless heart.

Ilia Delio, OSF
Georgetown University

This volume of poems by Fr. Larry Gosselin, OFM of *Unshadowed Light* is a book that one can easily read again and again, and each time the poems will give a deeper and more beautiful meaning. Fr. Larry's poetry explains Catholic teaching not in a documentary way, but in a way which opens our hearts at a profound spiritual level. We seem to be praying, rather than reading.

Fr. Kenan Osborne, OFM
Past President of the Catholic Theological Society of America
Past President of the Franciscan School of Theology, Berkeley, CA
Theologian and Author

"When my mind begins to darken and my shivering heart longs for something more or something other, writing helps because in the magic of words seeking each other and rubbing their surfaces together gently, a warmth emerges until striking each other sharply, a flame is struck from their surfaces, revealing some hidden fire within. And when it happens, though it's happened before, it is a surprise. I merely brought the words together, trying different combinations and discarding those soft words that haven't enough flint for sparking. And if I am lucky enough to strike a fire, my mind is lit up and my heart is warmed; and others who read the words join me at the fire. And there around that fire civilization continues."

By Fr. Murray Bodo, OFM

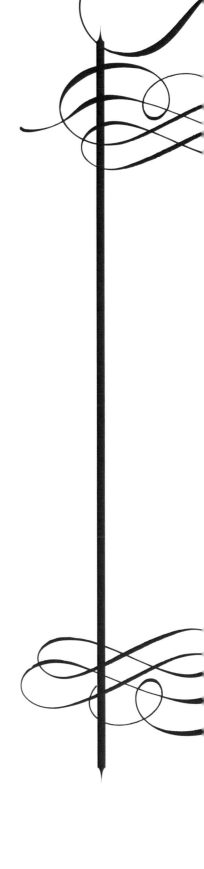

*Dedicated to
poets and people
of passion, in whose
steps we seek to walk,
and in whose words
we dare to speak
words of light.
Sts. Francis
and Clare*

"…for He (Jesus) will bring to light
what is hidden in the darkness…"
—I Corinthians 4:5 (a)

As revealed in the unshadowed light
of Saint Bernard of Clairvaux.
For all who pray and live in
"The Valley of Light"
'Clairvaux'.

And in honor of the
Communion of Saints

"Spirited light in
the secret darkness."
"Light for her people and time."
"Loving tenderness abounds for all."

—Hildegard of Bingen
Doctor of the Church

The above borrowed from the Apostolic Letter Proclaiming Saint Hildegard, professed nun of the order of Saint
Benedict, a Doctor of the Church, by Pope Benedict XVI, on October 7, 2012: "Light for her people and time."

Contents

Shadows

Light

Advent

Witness

The Work of God Increase

A Surprising Radiance

A Preface by the Editor

Opening the pages of this book, you will find poems of praise for the contemplative side of being. Father Larry's tireless devotion to uplifting and rallying the spirits of all who come to recognize God's divine love, will cherish the communion he shares with beloved Saint Francis of Assisi and Saint Clare.

However, beyond the multifaceted focus of this book of visionary poems, photographs and art, perhaps you will also find a common theme for peace shared with that of his Holiness, Pope Francis, whose purity of purpose speaks in concord with Saints Francis and Clare and so many others. Indeed, being "an instrument of peace," Pope Francis chose his papal name to reflect the Franciscan will to strive for harmony in a world up to its neck in brutality and war, just as was the case in St. Francis's time. Indeed, we must recall that the humble saint risked his own life by venturing to Damietta, Egypt during the Fifth Crusade and seeking out the Sultan Malik al-Kamel with the intention to peaceably end the strife there, to awaken the reigning sultan of that era to Christ.

We are not removed from the same turmoil, even if distanced by the years. For in recent days, with the urge to overpower others, cruelty of the most insidious and despicable kind has overrun every human effort to bring peace to the Middle East. And Pope Francis, in his pilgrimage of hope and good-will to the Holy Land, has spent most of his precious time having to state the obvious to anyone paying attention: "More than once we have been on the verge of peace (he said during his Holy Land tour), but the evil one, employing a variety of means, has succeed in blocking it." Simon Peres of Israel and Mahmoud Abbas both recognize that the people of Palestine and Israel are "aching for peace," and yet, for all their outward intentions, inward resentments and rage persist. The same holds forth between Russia and the Ukraine, and in Syria, Iraq and in Afghanistan. What remedy have we then that peace may flourish in our world?

Delivering us from evil is a delicate task. It requires a deeper resonance within our hearing, in our digesting of the voice of those inspired by God, and by force of the will of God's love to shift ourselves from negativity and despair, to a state of inner-peace and uncommon tranquility.

Easier said than done, you say.

Yet, in reflecting during quiet times on the inspired visions and concepts expressed in *Unshadowed Light,* and in other works of divine influence, one comes away with a wealth of hope for the salvation of the world. It is in what we deeply will ourselves to recognize, to comprehend, to believe, that we are urged to reconcile our relationship to God, and by so doing to finally be gifted with the nerve to wage peace in this world.

—Miki Landseadel

Fr. Larry Gosselin, OFM

About *Unshadowed Light*

The One Who Walks Silently

One evening I was on my way to a theater concert in downtown Santa Barbara and preparing to enjoy glorious music performed by the London Philharmonic Orchestra. I had been making my way through a narrow walkway close behind a couple who were also, apparently, heading to the same concert. Hurrying and wanting to pass them by, yet out of a sense of courtesy, I chose to stay behind and calculate whether I should indeed pass them or linger in the background and simply walk more slowly.

As I wandered in this "in-between," liminal space, all of a sudden a perfect portal appeared before me, and so I made a quick rush, which allowed me to quietly pass them by. After taking the lead, I caught the eye of the elderly gentleman behind me who had just been escorting his wife in front of me. He actually looked quite surprised and a little nonplused by my sudden appearance in front of them, noticing, in that moment, this hidden stranger who had slipped in front of them so stealthily.

For my part, I felt quite gleeful at how subtly I had maneuvered myself, how very hidden and silent I had been.

Yet, the gentleman turned to me and remarked, "Oh…I thought you were my shadow. Though I had seen movement in my periphery, you tread so silently that I must have confused you for my shadow."

I beamed at him, "No, I am certainly not a shadow; I am 'unshadowed', if you will, and I am real, even though I do seem to walk quietly beside you."

As you entertain the prospect of opening this book of poetry and of prayers, I would like to think of the "unshadowed one" from this perspective: as "the one who walks quietly," who is no longer hidden by darkness but who appears as the "unshadowed one." This is someone real who walks beside you. Saint Clare is that person. Though she may be hidden in the shadow of Saint Francis of Assisi, she is nevertheless real. She is the one who stands, often unnoticed, beside the Poverello, Francis, with her strong, loving and intuitive presence. She has no intention to pass him by, but wishes to be at his side in her quiet, significant way.

The One without Shadow

From modern psychological analysis we have become familiar with speaking about "the shadow side" of an individual. This "persona" reflects a place of some dark, secret, forbidden and generally concealed part of a person's intentionality or rationality. When we speak of "the shadow side," we're associating it with an unconscious motivation that lingers as a kind of harbor of wrongful justification within a person. Contrast this with "the unshadowed one": a person of purity having no devious or secretive intentions. In an example of one such individual, we have Nathanael, the Apostle of Jesus, of whom Jesus said, "Truly, this one is a pure Israelite; in this one there is no guile." Thus, the "unshadowed one" is an individual having no hidden agenda or false pretenses. Like Nathanael, this person is the purest of the pure.

As much as Nathanael represents a biblical paragon, so does Clare, whose name means "unshadowed light." As a pure light, I hope you will meet not only St. Clare of the ages, but the purity of purity that remains as a "hidden sweetness" within the vastness of your own being.

Welcome to this place where we can walk together.
Here, indeed, we're endowed with *unshadowed light!*

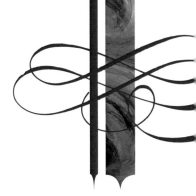

Fr. Larry Gosselin, OFM

Who was St. Clare of Assisi?

The person to best answer this question would be Thomas of Celano, the author of *First Life of Francis of Assisi,* who wrote his account of St. Francis between 1228 and 1230 A.D., when Clare was about thirty-six years of age. Here we know Clare as the prioress of the little church of San Damiano, which Francis rebuilt, stone upon stone, and where Clare lived cloistered for the remainder of her life after her conversion.

Celano describes Clare as such:

> "This is the blessed and holy place where the glorious religion and most excellent Order of Poor Ladies and holy virgins had its happy beginning, about six years after the conversion of the blessed Francis and through that same blessed man. The Lady Clare, a native of the city of Assisi, the most precious and strongest stone of the whole structure, stands as the foundation for all the other stones. After the beginning of the Order of Brothers, when this lady was converted to God through the counsel of the holy man, she lived for the good of many and as an example to countless others. Noble by lineage, but more noble by grace, chaste in body, most chaste in mind, young in age, mature in spirit, steadfast in purpose and most eager in her desire for divine love, endowed with wisdom and excelling in humility, bright in name, more brilliant in life, most brilliant in character."

May Saint Clare lead you, stone by stone, into her dwelling, as your holy place, where her unshadowed light resides in brilliance.

—Fr. Larry Gosselin, OFM

Fr. Larry Gosselin, OFM

Risk Everything; the Soul is Made for Joy

Ascending, clad with pure light,
as if brother Sun and Sister Fire
had inflamed the heart of Francis,
stigmatic, seraphic wings appeared
imprinting "El Poverello" with joy.
The Poor Man had risked everything,
found himself Mirrored in Perfection.

We are all made for joy,
given a pure heart, soaring spirit,
to be lifted to light in Christ
that inflames each soul,
lifts the spirit
to love.

Lord, we cannot dance
unless you teach us.
We want to leap joyfully;
lead us to risk…joy.

On the Occasion of the Commemoration of the Death of St. Francis of Assisi

To all,
Sisters and Brothers in Christ through Francis,
Loving and fraternal greetings to you on this blessed day of
Our Seraphic Holy Father Francis.

As we walk in the footprints of this Poor Man of Assisi,
may we find great joy, comfort and peace,
as well as challenge, effort and zeal,
by living and proclaiming
the Kingdom of God.

I find great inspiration in the prophetic words
of Our Holy Father, Pope Francis's homily today…
"Praised, may you be, Most High, All Powerful God, Good Lord…
by all your creatures."
Indeed, these proclaim the first words of *St. Francis's Canticle*:
"Love for all creation, for its harmony."

St. Francis of Assisi bears witness to the need to respect all that God has created,
and that men and women are called to safeguard and protect,
but above all he bears witness to respect and love for every human being.
God created the world to be a place where
harmony and peace can flourish.
Harmony and Peace!

Francis was just such a man.
From this City of Peace, I repeat with all the strength and meekness of love:
Let us respect creation.
Let us not be instruments of destruction!
Let us respect each human being.
May there be an end to armed conflicts which cover the earth in blood;
may the clash of arms be silenced;
and everywhere, may hatred yield to love,

Fr. Larry Gosselin, OFM

injury to pardon,
and discord to unity.
Let us listen to the cry of all those who are weeping,
who are suffering and who are dying
because of violence, terrorism or war
in the Holy Land
so dear to St. Francis
in Syria,
throughout the Middle East and everywhere in the world.

We turn to you, Francis, and we ask you
obtain for us God's gift of harmony and peace in our world.
"Lord Jesus Christ, Father of Mercies,
do not look upon our ingratitude, but always keep in mind
the surpassing goodness you have shown this city, Assisi.
Grant that it may be the home of men and women who know you in truth
and who glorify Your Most Holy and Glorious Name,
now and for all ages. Amen.

Let this be the Mirror of Perfection

Dear friends in Christ,
May the peace and joy of St. Francis proclaimed to all people and for all creation,
dwell in your hearts today and always.
Happy feast day, one and all!

—October 4, 2013, Assisi, Italy

Unshadowed Light
A Franciscan Contemplative

If the world suddenly stopped,
and sense of all we were faded into darkness,
all flesh would become a Word…
Word spoken as Light in the eternal darkness.

Flesh must be made anew, by Word,
for all comes to good in love, from the Light.
Our words made of spirit,
our songs fall to Light the sweetened fields.

Forgive me for my sheer delight,
my reflection upon the Spirit of God a'birthing.
But here, in the darkness of earth,
we are companions of the Light that always rises.

I see a gentle hill to rest upon,
which lies in the place of stillness within the soul.
Full of Light, it warms the body
in ardor, grace, work, and loss; we belong.

Such a song sung alone, but in harmony,
echoes the cry of all creation coming to birth,
searching for its own belonging, where to abide,
it turns quietly to the cohesive wholeness.

As if to go walking in a dark valley
one arrives in morning Light above the high hills,
arising from the shadows of thoughts,
entering upon a bountiful spring of new life.

Just set aside a place to sit down…sit down!
Be quiet now. Depend upon reflection here.
Knowing the inspiration of growing older,

Fr. Larry Gosselin, OFM

accept the rest that comes in peace, in stillness.

All creation speaks to us in quietude.
In silence, prayers prayed return back to the prayerful.
Stop and praise the speechless starlight.
Stop for a while and praise.

Be like the river that flows quietly
to a destination rising far beyond the distant shore.
Be with all who remain still and nameless;
in quietude give each one a name: your own.

A Vision of the Poor Lady Without Shadow
Rendered in the style of Scott Cairns
From his *The Theology of Delight*

Imagine a meadow.

About you a little tentative world blooms.

There, in that space, a new world opens.

Clouds dim the sky,

but not the sunburst that floods forth its rich beam of light

upon a nearby field of grazing sheep,

wandering in a wide,

green field with great delight.

A pasture of wildflowers forms in this fashion,

of the tentative world before you,

shimmering.

Now, in the mind's eye, see—a woman appears.

She stands tall, her long trek leading her here,

to this unshaded spot of the field.

In one hand she holds up a monstrance,

and like the sunburst, its facets radiate light.

Lifting her other hand,

she reaches forward and gently waves to you.

The tall lady in her worn robe stands not far from where you sit,

and you smile back.

You both enjoy the coolness of this place,

delighting in the rustic scene,

watching over sheep as the wind rustles the wildflowers.

You get up to sit closer; your movement startles the flock.

They seem to scatter—

Except for one: a lamb.

It holds itself up, unafraid, free of the others.

Then, for no apparent reason,

it begins to scamper, prancing,

then leaping all about the field.

You, the two watchers, observe with delight,

with celebration!

Like an invitation to a wedding,

Fr. Larry Gosselin, OFM

witnessing the joyous dance of the lamb
as light plays upon the open field.
You turn and the lady waves again but now from afar,
yet you find yourself holding the weight
of the monstrance in your hand:
a memory you knew,
yet to happen.

Prayer of Solomon

Was I just asleep?
Awakening in gentleness
in the soft patter of birdsong,
came enduring morning light.
Surely the daybreak will be quiet.
In sunrise peace, for which I long, sighs
a probing question, "What is it that you want?"
"Ask something of Me, and I will give it to you."
And so I answered,
"O Lord, my God, You made me and You know me.
Search my soul and discern what it is I need to ask.
Give me Your wisdom with a pure, understanding heart,
so I may lead Your people to distinguish rightly what is good."
The Lord said,
"All things work for good for all who love that which is godly.
According to divine purpose, you are to seek that which is Mine.
I give you my heart, wise in understanding, skilled at fine judgment,
sagely knowing my commands. Yes…you do love my commands.
Do you understand all of these things?
Consider.
"The kingdom of Heaven is like a treasure buried in a field,
which one finds, and out of joy, sells all that it possesses."
What an enduring heirloom! Such is a pearl of great price
brought forth from the storeroom of old and new.
You will receive these pearls of wisdom. So now
take them from your mind and heart. Receive!
From a place of governance, let all know
that I shall lead my people in wisdom.

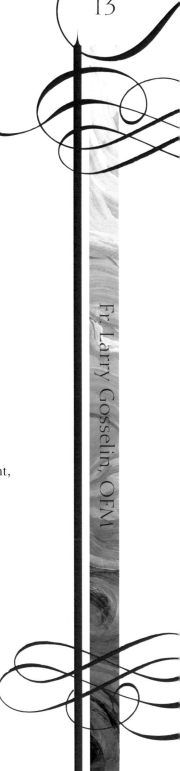

Fr. Larry Gosselin, OFM

Shadows

Waiting upon the glimmer of day,
wade through the shadows.
Casting aside hints of darkness,
Ease into eternal light.

An Introduction to Shadows

Dear Reader,

The *Prayer of St. Francis* has been sung and offered as an enduring proclamation of his being "An Instrument of Peace." Although the words of this prayer were never inscribed by St. Francis, its message captures his gently compelling spirituality.

In this section, wherein we directly face the "Shadows," I offer you a similar rendering of what might be described as St. Francis's *contemplative shadow*: St. Clare, however, given expression here as the "Prayer of St. Clare." For following each poem in the next series you'll see an excerpt from St. Clare's original writings, expressed as either an admonition or recommendation offered to her sisters and taken from the *Letters of St. Clare.*

In their own writings or in the reportage concerning these two saints, not many recorded examples indicate the ways in which Francis and Clare perceived things from the same viewpoint. But one understanding that can certainly be cited is the loving way they looked upon their beloved, Jesus.

Indeed, it was Christ, fragile and defenseless and given into human hands, as at Bethlehem, that defined their shared and common vision. For Clare the monstrance of the Eucharist was the icon of her life. Thus she heard a voice "like a child" coming from the sacred vessel assuring her: "I will protect you always."

And so now, with incredible presumption, I would like to set before you what might be a meditation on St. Clare's writings, identified as a *Prayer of St. Clare* and propose her to be an "Instrument of Light." I ask you to imagine that Francis is sending Clare and her sisters his child-like "canticle-testament" by saying:

"Listen, little poor ones
called by the Lord,
who have come together
from many parts and provinces.
Do not look at the life without,
for the life of the Spirit is better."

Fr. Larry Gosselin, OFM

Shadows

Shadows of night
hold no darkness
to a heart in gloom.
Love, as love, is born
when we grieve over it.
"The people who walked in darkness have seen a great light;
upon those who dwell in the land of gloom, a light has shone."
Once an exile begins
your eyes will seek out
light of the day, in night,
as moon, casting shadows
illuminates hidden visions.
"For the yoke that burdened",
has now been shattered, as on
that gloriously bright Midian day.
Light speaks, assuming a new way.
"Stay with me now in night vision."
Hold the light.
Illuminate night.
Shadows residing,
the light presiding,
in unshadowed light.

—Book of the Prophet Isaiah 8:23-9-3

Artistic work of Amedee Gosselin,
Grandfather, dated 1887

Shadow of Death

All that lives,
lives under
the shadow of death.

All having been born
have put a foot
inside its door.

Put the other foot
into
life's door as light,
grace,
mystery of wonder
beyond,

overcome with pure
light
dim shadows dissolve.

I give thanks to the Giver of Life
From whom every good thing proceeds.
He has lifted you with splendor and beauty.
And He sees only goodness in you.
And one thing more I say to you,
As your Mother, as a sister, as your friend,
Remember your life's journey
And follow through to its end."

—Admonition of St. Clare

Fr. Larry Gosselin, OFM

Shadow of Hatred

"Listen to Me, O islands,
And pay attention people from afar.
The Lord called Me from the womb;
from the body of my mother,
He named Me.
Can a mother forget her nursing child,
and have no compassion for the child of her womb?"
Isaiah 49:1,15

When the dark night enters,
and love becomes just a distant word,
blindness walks in the shadow of hatred.
When the night comes in,
darkness becomes a staff;
it comes in with strength,
the power to destroy love.
There in the dark of night,
Blindness, as sleepwalking
love and hatred each face
the other.
Have you forgotten my name?

"Cling to His sweet Mother
who carried Him within.
Though all the heavens are too small,
your body is His home.
Follow His footprints gently,
with good and humble heart,
and you will hold within your soul
the treasure that is life.
And love Him totally,
who gave Himself for your love.
And you will hold Him
Who holds all things in truth.
And you will hold Him."

—Admonition of St. Clare

Fr. Larry Gosselin, OFM

Stilling the Shadow of Greed

"O blessed Poverty,
To those who love her ways
She gives the riches of the endless
Life of God."

"Share your bread with the hungry,
Shelter the oppressed and the homeless;
Clothe the naked when you see them,
Do not turn your back on your own.
Then your light shall break forth like the dawn."

"Then light shall rise for you in the darkness,
and gloom shall become for you like midday."

Then…
Let love be love in life,
Let light be light in love,
Let light be love in living.

"Do not look at the life in this world.
Do not look at the life outside.
The life of the spirit is better.
The life of the spirit is true.
I promise
that each one of you will have
a crown as a heavenly queen
with the Virgin Mary.
through the merits
of Mother Clare.
And so be it.
Amen."

The Prophet Isaiah 58:7, 10
—Admonition of St. Clare

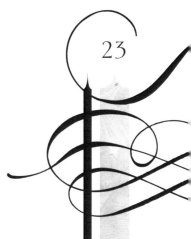

The Shadow of Misunderstanding

I am not.
You are not.
Understanding.

I am not I.
You are not you.
Misunderstanding.

I am not the one
walking beside you.
You are not the one I see.
All I see is this shadow.

Yet

May we talk, gently. Forgive, silently.
Remain standing with each other, seeing the light.

Fr. Larry Gosselin, OFM

"Look upon His heart
Which opens to you each day.
Though He was despised,
The lowest of all.
Look upon His sacred cross,
Which brings life again.
Gaze upon His life.
Gaze upon His love.
Gaze upon His coming through
From Heaven above.
From Heaven above."

—Admonition of St. Clare

Shadow of Bitterness

"The soldiers also mocked Him,
coming up to Him,
offering Him
bitter gall,
saying

'If you are the King of the Jews, save Yourself.'"
Luke 23:36-37

Gall
"bitterness to endure,
suffocating of spirit."

Bitterness is a mirror
in which you see yourself
staring blindly, as if in shadow,
as on a trapeze, swinging, flailing away
unable to let go, locked, dangling in midair,
held up, opened, as if on a cross, arms pinioned.

Let go—Let God hold you as you fall into His arms of mercy.

Fr. Larry Gosselin, OFM

Unshadowed Light

"If you open to life's pains,
then with Him you shall reign,
and allow your heart to grieve,
then with Him you shall rejoice.
Open to His cross, the wounds of each day's love.
Then you shall know the splendor of His Kingdom above."

—Admonition of St. Clare

Shadow of Dread

Word held in the throat
Buried as violent duty.
Forsaken, fearful.
Wishing to
be no
sign of
l
o
v
e
"It was during that time
that a serious disturbance broke out
in connection with the Way."
Acts 19:23

If one dreads to give love,
one is saying
"For God's sake, go alone."

But bright beauty can be kindled again.
Remember the inscription on the soul.

Fr. Larry Gosselin, OFM

Unshadowed Light

"Called by the Lord,
You have been gathered together.
I beg you, in my love for you,
that you use with kindness
what the Lord gives to you."

—Admonition of St. Clare

Facing the Shadow of Sadness

All strive
For "The Pursuit of Happiness"…
Quiet elation
embedded in the soul.
We have lingering hope,
believe in one's goodness.
No need to contain
inner happiness.
Hold it! Share it!
Endless possibilities for love.

But
in sadness,
keep some faith to rub against.
When joyless, freedom
To hold, to mold, and stay bold.
Raise hands;
you see joy flows with every touch.
Happiness floats,
flies a swift pace.
Light steps
sing
neither
keeping down
nor
muffling
the voice within.

Fr. Larry Gosselin, OFM

"What you hold may you always hold.
What you do may you always do.
Go forward secure and with joy,
on the path of happiness.
With swift pace
and light step
go freely."

—Admonition of St. Clare

Shadow of Fear

"I will always protect you!"
The Voice of the Lord, as spoken to St. Clare

Her own voice came as light
composed as simply a soft stare
of confidence in the face of fear.
In her heart she held the naïve light,
blessed as truth, fearless as new delight.
Uncontested, fear scattered into seamless air.
A stance, stare of love, gazed so simply, entirely clear.

*"I assure you, daughters that you will suffer no evil;
only have faith in Christ."*
The voice of St. Clare as spoken to her sisters

What more can be said?
How can one draw back the voice spoken?
Walk by day, as you walk by dawn, in pure confidence!
Keep this as your warmth; do this as you're walking, living, sleeping.
In life's rough and tumble ways, hold firm and peer into His heart.

*"If you open to life's pains
then with Him you shall reign
and allow your heart to grieve,
then with Him you will rejoice.
Open to His cross, wounds of each day's love.
You will see the splendor of His Kingdom above.*

*Gaze upon His life…
Gaze upon His love…
Gaze upon his coming
from Heaven above.*

—Based on the admonitions of St. Clare
and the story of St. Clare defending Assisi
against the attack of the Saracens

Fr. Larry Gosselin, OFM

Shadow of Gloom

Eyes are compelled to witness
shadows of gloom.
But, whispering in the darkness
dawns a new destiny.
Discerning through these shadows,
one sees lights' glimmer.
Daylight sets aside the shroud of night,
as its shadow side.
Light sets asunder the dreary gloom,
bearing it away peacefully.
Filled with your splendor and beauty
every good proceeds.
Come! Come! Come! Into this new light,
secure in joy.
Make yourself beautiful, daughter of God,
for the One who is life,
Whose gentleness is peace
Whose heart inflames love,
Whose grace is all we want.
Let nothing ever dissuade you
from living such purity in life.
Dispel all harsh shadows of gloom.
See only goodness.

—Based on the Admonitions of St. Clare to her sisters

Shadow of Doubt

"You can't pray a lie," said Huckleberry Finn.

For

daylight and dreaming minds
awaken to a spectrum of light certitude,
whence enters a nearly limitless shadow of doubt,
that echoes a barrage of betrayal in an ocean of darkness.
Prayer for lost things, dispossessed, circling asunder with vacant indifference.

"You can't pray a lie," said Huckleberry Finn

A liturgy of lost things emerges despite
rising pools of the depths and shallows of doubt.
Splintering light, swirls steadily, directly, unfathomably skyward.
You wait anxiously, while a fervent claimed prayer flies forward in hope.
"Why?" you ask. Ask Job, who burning from a million unseen brands spoke it.

Light resurfacing casts out all shadows of doubt.

"You can't pray a lie," said Huckleberry Finn.

Fr. Larry Gosselin, OFM

Light

"O lamps of fire bright-burning
with wondrous brilliance, turning
deep caverns of my soul to pools of light!
Once shadowed, dim, unknowing
now their new-found glowing
gives warmth and radiance for my Love's delight.
Ah! gentle and so loving
you wake with me, proving
that you are there in secret and alone;
your fragrant breathing stills me,
your grace, your glory fills me
so tenderly your love becomes my own."

—St. John of the Cross

Mothers of Light
Mary, the Mother of the Lord
Ortolana, Mother of Clare

Light piercing in luminous silence,
glows in a mother's face…
gleaming forth the fair countenance.
She gently cradles the child of her womb.
Moment and life experience in one word,
pouring forth the unforgettable sweetness in her smile.
Pure delight issues from soft eyes viewing the babe.
"Can a mother ever forget her infant,
or be without tenderness
for the child of her womb?
Even should she forget,
I will never forget you."

"While she, the mother of Clare, lay in her confinement,
the pregnant woman feared greatly. Yet, as she prayed,
a voice sounded in her ears:
'Do not be afraid;
you've been given a divine gift.
You will give birth to a Light
whose new glow
will enlighten the world.'
Complying to these words,
she named the child Clare
for the clear, light flow
of sacred water."

—Versified legend of the Virgin Clare

Fr. Larry Gosselin, OFM

Sweet Fragrance
of Unshadowed Light

"Clare,

brilliant by her bright merits,

by the brightness of her great glory in Heaven,

and by the luminance of her sublime miracles on earth,

shines radiantly.

It should not be surprising

that a light so enkindled,

so illuminating

could not be kept hidden

without shining brightly,

giving brilliant light

in the house of the Lord;

nor could a vessel filled

with perfume be concealed

so it would not reveal fragrance

and suffuse the Lord's house

with sweetness."

—The Papal Decree of Canonization
Pope Alexander IV
August 15, 1255

Zarin*

Pure as golden light
illuminates rays from
the brilliance of the sun.
So the Light of God's Son,
Jesus, radiates as a shining
golden light
hidden
not by night
sparkles
ever bright
dwells
celestial white
sweetly
cloistered aright
in Clare.

*Zarin means golden in Armenian

Fr. Larry Gosselin, OFM

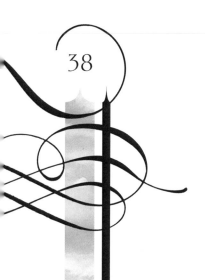

Woman of Tender Love

"I am speaking to my blessed soul"

Said the Poor Lady, Clare, to her sisters,
"Do you see the King of Glory, whom I see?"
The hand of the Lord was placed upon her,
as she received a joyful vision beyond her eyes.
"I am speaking to my blessed soul," said Clare.
**"Go without anxiety
for you have a good
escort on your journey."**

As a mother sees her child,
she saw a glorious escort
standing not far off.

Another sister saw
a multitude of virgins in white garments,
one more splendid than the others, walk among them.
One appeared to carry a latticed thurible*. Such splendor!
It turned the night within the house into daylight.
On the day after the feast of St. Lawrence,
the body of Clare was covered and
the bridal bed decorated.
And that most blessed soul
departed to be crowned.

—August 11, 1253

*a censer

The Death of Death

Here a new horizon rose
vertically in the ground.
Arms extending to reach
all creation in new hope.
The Word of God came to be hung upon the cross of death so to bring life.
The death of death became the life of life in the year thirty-three at Calvary.
A costly prized gift that lifts all creation into the unconditional love of God.
Behold the wood of the Cross, may all be beholding, the wood of the Cross.
The Lord of life observed here in a new horizon of life.
Outstretched arms bestow on all pure redeeming grace.
Here behold, the living God, who lifts us all in peace.
May all creation taste the hidden sweetness of His love.

Death, you have died to life;
Life, you are lifted to glory.
All, held as one, in this One,
given new life to live in love.
Lift high upon this Cross,
all in the divine wood of life,
the hope of creation uplifted.
Most High, O Glorious God,
lighten the darkness of heart.
Give right faith as sure as hope,
Perfect Love by understanding
Your commandment: to love.

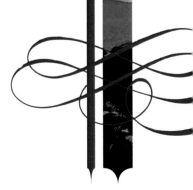

Fr. Larry Gosselin, OFM

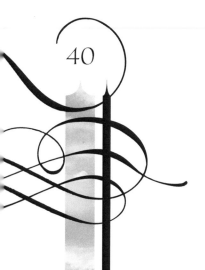

They Shall Dart About as Sparks Through the Stubble

"In the time of visitation
they shall shine and
shall dart about as
sparks through
the stubble."
Shine on!
This love marriage,
calls us to be chosen,
living fully with new life.
Imagine, abundantly new
loving, while in love eternally.
What creature living under God
would not take that gift in flight
Heavenward on the wings of love?
Forward ascending, as sparkling embers
darting, shimmering from the Master's fire;
the Soul rises up in the Resurrection of the Just.

—Book of Wisdom 3:7

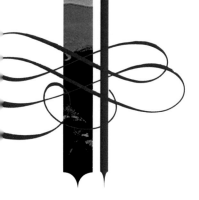

Sun Shine, Son Shine

To
each day
the gift of light
arises with new life.
Ages past, infinite silence,
remembering eternity expanding
sweetly, shining, as if upon an ocean.
A day has dawned; a people are reborn,
who witness the sun, Son shining above.
Rise in golden splendor, O Shining One!
The hallowed day rises with healing rays
blazing like an oven of flying embers.
You love us into your own new light.
Son shine as morning sun shines.
Vein a flood that is fed by fire,
illuminating a holy people
shining in a new day.
Arise, Light Divine!
"Breath of Day"
shine on!
Break the darkness of the night.

—Based on the Prophet Malachi 3:19-20

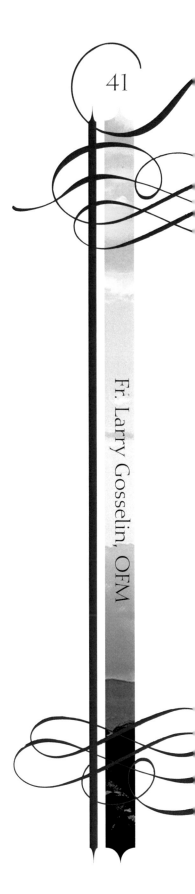

Fr. Larry Gosselin, OFM

Love Growing in Me

When night asks
Who are you? I answer,
"I am your very own, born in you.
I have come to life in the dark womb of love,
and welcomed in birth, held in the warm arms of love.
This, art of the soul, harvests a deeper life through the light of love.
The body is the soul, as the soul is the body,
coming from life, born into light.
Who is this one who welcomes me?
What is this source of life and love?
In whose flow of life and cherishing
have I been formed, brought forth?
What name may I cry out?
What place was I within?
What word the first I heard?
These questions grow in me
as have I in her.

She is Mother:
this one name,
source of life,
for we are one.
You living in me,
me living in you.

A Retinue of a Hundred Thousand Golden Eagles

They flew in one accord
above the crowd of onlookers.
An artistic configuration in the sky,
assembled, they spoke to the awakened ones.
Nothing in the sky was broken, lost, torn, incomplete,
only pure eagle wings beating nobly in the sky.
Light kindled golden as late leaves of fall
in ceaseless measure float, descend.
In that hour it seemed the sun
glowed behind a shadow
of day at dawn's brink.
Fly, fly, fly
You are
to be
Flight.

Fr. Larry Gosselin, OFM

Prepare the Place

He needs a place.
We need a place to lay him.
Let us place him here in the cave.
He will rest in this carved out place in peace.

He came to this place,
this place of death and sorrow.
He prayed for him in the place of death.
In this place He raised him up and out, beyond.

Lazarus, come out of this place.
For I come to this place that is not death.
Come out of this place! Come out of this place!
Believe in a land beyond death, a place of new hope.

And so He prayed and taught us
to pass from this place to the new one.
Come to this place! Come to *this* place! All of you!
Roll back the stone! Break forth the vault! Open the grave!

Prepare yourself for this place of rest.
Here you lay, not in death, but in eternal life.
Come to this place! Come to *this* place! All of you!
Remove the burial linens, untie yourself and stand forth free!

For you are free here in this place,
free to live, to move and have your being.
Come anew to this place! Come to *this* place! Come anew!
Let the filth of death be removed, replaced with the fresh fragrance of life.

Fr. Larry Gosselin, OFM

Advent

Color of Light

Blue.
The color of light
Blue sky as blue ocean
Shadowing depth, reflecting further
Inviting to the distant
Stillness in color
The Word,
was, is
will be,
coming.
Advent,
as blue,
always
as new.

Fr. Larry Gosselin, OFM

Hidden Light

In the silent foliage of night
resides the black water of silence.
Above the deep current flickers a light:
sparkling glimmers of hope, from
a hidden light in the darkness.
Joy like a white dove flies
into the stillness
of waiting.

Announcing

Chosen One,
be not afraid
for unto you a
child is given.

Birthing

Thus given to you
to bring to birth
a long awaited Word
growing in you, with you.

To All

The Transcendent One Speaks
as the Transparent One
announcing peace
light and joy
to all.

Forecasting Joy

Upon the page of life,
exists a word of light
written by the hand of joy
sustaining constant renewal.

My friend, you are beautiful today!
But then, when are you not beautiful?
Something lovely yet hidden about you
always rises as the moon, skyward, beyond.

You are like the pure milkweed urging joy to life,
descending over the resting, cocooned butterfly larva,
saying: "Stand up! Open your opulent, multi-colored wings!"
The sky's the limit and you were made to fly lightly, forecasting joy.

Fr. Larry Gosselin, OFM

Turning darkness into burning light
Burning swords to turning plowshares

Turning and burning!
Here we come into the light,
beating swords into plowshares,
and the spears into pruning hooks.
Expectant, we know we are to hope
in the light, awakened and returning.
Quiet days, here in our primeval cradle.
How long to wait? As we long to wake?
"The days are coming," says the Lord.
Let us walk in the light of the Lord."
"Yes, the day is coming, is near!"
Winter fire, light in darkness,
Violet, Rose, Evergreens.
Joy in stillness…
Hope in peace,
Awaits us here!
God is coming!
Light awaits us!
Light awakes us!
Here, in the light!

—First Sunday of Advent

Advent of Light

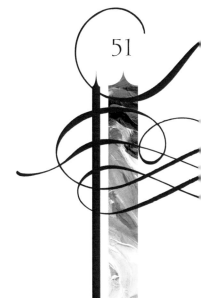

In the beginning all was blue,
and the blue was the night:
the night ineffable blue.
Darkness, too, was blue.
Light born
into blue.
All things came
from a truth of blue,
a hue that enlightens all.
In the lasting hours of darkness
I have watched, waited through the night,
in an upper room through long blue windows,
four candles, purple, pink and burning through the night.
I have imagined the comings and goings of years past and present,
of loved voices that spoke of forgotten heralds with no pictures past—
only their enduring ancient voices
bespeaking Hope
Peace! Joy! Light!
Season of Light
born new
in blue.
Something old…
something new,
something borrowed
from innocence in blue.
The marriage of light to darkness
proclaimed, invoked by eternal silence.
All waiting, longing, hoping, anticipating
in expectation of light revealed within the night.
O, Come! Long Awaited One, Come! Root of Jesse,
Come! Wisdom from on High; Come! Thou Key of David,
Come! Thou Dayspring from on High; Come! Desire of Nations.
O Come, O Come Emmanuel, and ransom captive Israel, all who weep
in lonely exile steeped in blue, waiting for the Son of God to appear anew.

Fr. Larry Gosselin, OFM

Advent by Night
Hoping Light in the Darkness

It is not the night; it's the world

that seems to have fallen into darkness.

Console yourself in the coming of new light.

It will return; listen for dawn with keen expectation.

It appears like the high sea—plain and calm—at the spring tide.

Light comes—hear with your eyes; see with your ears.

Let go of trepid fear that hovers in the dark shadows.

This is life: listen, see—the living spring sings

a song of new life, joy, peace, hope.

Its flame flickers in a blue hue.

Daylight comes

as a child

at birth

cries

with

joy.

Fr. Larry Gosselin, OFM

Rejoice, the Steppe Blooms!

The history of light
like a heavenly constellation
presses forward, ahead at full speed
illuming generations after generations.

Parched lands exult.
The steppe will bloom! Rejoice!
Eyes of the blind, the ears of the deaf
will be opened and cleared to see and hear.

"Comfort, give comfort
to my people," says the Lord.
"Rejoice in the Lord always! I say Rejoice!"
Be strong, fear not! He comes with vindication.

The Coming One
reaches out a hand to you,
He's crowned with everlasting joy. Sing!
"His love and mercy endures forever and ever!"

Sorrow flees
at the sound of His coming.
Ransomed, returned, we are in light.
Be patient! "Prepare the Way of the Lord!"

The farmer waits,
precious fruit of earth to appear.
In stillness and hope, we await new life,
crowned in glory bearing gladness and everlasting joy.

Rejoice!
Again, I say rejoice!
Rose-colored Advent candle
lights our longing into expectant joy.

—On the third Sunday of Advent—Gaudete Sunday

"Umbra Demonstrat Lucem*"
In the shadow of dawn,
light came into the darkness.

"Illuminare"
Light from Light
Clearer than light
Word became flesh
and dwelt among us.
No shadow of darkness
could dispel the radiance.
Shadows revealing a Light
This day, child of light is born.
Cradle, Cross, light, darkness.
Gloria en Excelsis Deo!

"Admonitio"
Look into the mirror.
Learn how to give light.
All that is, is ours in God.
We, permanent beginners,
delivered unto light in light.
Clear unshadowed light, born,
shining in the House of the Lord.
Into a heart's night comes a way.
You, born this day are new in Christ.
Gloria en Excelsis Deo!

*"It is the shadow which reveals the light."
—Poem etched into a sundial

Led to a Land the Wise Ones Know

How many stars have we to follow
navigating when, where, to arrive
to one seeking, the One sought?
Only seekers know the sought.
Only the sought are found.
Only the found revealed.
Follow! Follow! Follow!
O, star of destination,
light the night bright,
foreshadowing all
destinies to know.
Arid desert winds blow hard our bone-dry path.
Sunken footprints, harrowed in the sands, disappear.
Only the wise of heart, strong in spirit will endure.
Now camels need must feed, our apt task at hand.
We attend to things with a quiet flow of anticipation.
We are being led and must follow aware: Light of Light!
We are both the wise and the wanderer, that longs to see
through the darkness, night scrutiny and vision of a child.
Born to be King,
to offer Him our gifts.
Yes, Gold, Frankincense, Myrrh,
but mostly tendering our journey in finding
the One who led us to the land the wise ones know.

—Feast of the Epiphany

Fr. Larry Gosselin, OFM

The Prodigal Father, Joseph
"And his father saw him afar off"

Jesus,
my little
gentle son,
watching you
learning to walk
there in the garden
at home in Nazareth…
seeing you walk, talk
playing and praying here,
from our garden in Nazareth…
And so He prayed in the Garden
And His sweat became as drops of blood.
He prayed, "Abba, Father!"
Jesus,
my little
gentle son,
you must eat;
come to the table.
Take a cup and drink;
Receive, bread in plenty.
Your body needs rich food
so that you may feed others,
here, from our home in Nazareth.
This, my blood of the New Covenant, poured out.
This bread is living food, "Take it, this is my body."
He prayed "Abba, Father!"
Jesus
my little
gentle son,
I give my love
to and for you.
Before you I lay down
my life and love in devotion,
so that you might grow through me.
"And He said, "I will arise and go to my Father."
He prayed, "Abba, Father!"

I Come Baptizing You With Water,
He Comes Baptizing You in the Holy Spirit.

Jesus

He's my cousin,

my first cousin, on my

mother's side, through Mary.

I thought of him as someone special.

Jesus,

chosen by the Lord.

He was born filled with joy,

Jesus even made me leap with joy,

they said, *"When in my Mother's womb."*

Jesus,

as a young boy,

I went with him to Galilee.

I swam with him in the fresh water.

He said, *"This water is life giving for us."*

Jesus,

came to the river

to be baptized in the Jordan.

Again, He made me leap for joy.

But I felt unworthy to untie his sandal strap.

Jesus

said, *"Permit it now,*

for in this way it is fitting for us."

I then saw the heavens open and a dove—

"This is my beloved Son, in whom I am well pleased."

Jesus

said He heard it too

and seemed to be moved by the Spirit.

He went to the desert, where I come from.

I went to the city where He had been living before.

Fr. Larry Gosselin, OFM

Jesus

said, we must change.

"You must decrease, and I must increase."

In a mysterious way, again He made joy
leap within.

At the Sea of Galilee, He saw others and
said, *"Follow Me."*

Jesus,

I am merely a man,

"A voice crying out in the desert,

'Prepare the way of the Lord,

Make His paths straight."

Again, my heart leaps

with great

joy!

Who is to Come, the King?
The King Who is to Come!

Sovereignty rules supreme.
Creation gives glory,
people due honor;
all enhances
—All—
To the King!
To the King, all!
The rule of the King
proceeds eon upon eon,
crowned with stately laurel,
royalty enthrones noble victory.

The King comes.
Where are the lights?
Where are the wreaths?
Where is the decorated hall?
Open all the gates of the palace!
Let the King in for He comes to rule!

Now the King comes.
Descending from royal throne,
entering into a people's throng.
Behold! Before our eyes He stands,
opening locked portals of our hearts!
Let the King enter. Let Him reign in our
lives.

Come to the King.
in victory and in pain,
we come into his kingdom.
We feel a journey yet before us,
Crowned through power and might.
We enter, as you reign King of our hearts.

Sovereignty rules supreme.
Creation gives glory,
people due honor;
all enhances.
—All—
To the King!

Fr. Larry Gosselin, OFM

The Palette of the Master Artist

Radiant coloration
placed lovingly, separately,
held together by creation, within each one's own distinction.
In the mind of the Master Artist, such finite degrees combine grandly.
Though blended humbly, still uniquely their own.
Inward showings, brought forth to the surface,
merged as the One in their full spectrum and variation.
The mystery of each sublime color
creates an expression of love and intention,
each quality respected, upheld, honored for itself.
Such truth unknowable except for the clarity of the divine
as One in Three,
as love in Thee, the Other.
Yet, such ruminations keep us in their embrace
of the mutual and immense
Love.
To be in this love,
to be held
in this
complex
merging
as
One,
affirms we are One in Thee.

Witness

"All the soul's infirmities are brought to light; they are set before its eyes to be felt and healed.

Now, with the light and heat of the divine fire, I see and feel those weaknesses and miseries, which previously resided within, hidden and unfelt."

—St. John of the Cross

My Name is Matthew

Like a deer, or even its hunter,
you have to watch each morning, each and every day
for any movement in the brush
that can signify new changes upon the earth.
I have become "Like new wine in new wineskins."
The wine is now rich in flavor
for it has been aged in the cask of spiritual stillness.
I saw myself as a supplicant
and now I have become a disciple: Matthew, son of Alphaeus.

My name is Matthew, which means,
"Gift of God"
but no one thought of me being that.

I sat at a table collecting taxes,
kept records with parcel and pen, in my former life,
accounting those who had paid
the distasteful, distained and debilitating Roman tax.
Hated by all, but forced to obey,
I was feared, despised and denigrated by the Pharisees;
they called me a public sinner.
You might say, "I was dimned in the dark before dawn."
Publican was my given name.

I met this man, Jesus, who gave me a command:
"Come, follow Me!"
Now, in this call, I stand tall, not rejected, graced
with pen and parcel in hand.
His words of life emerge as new wine in a new way.
His words overwhelmed me,
caused me to be an evangelist, Matthew: to be a virtuous man.
The inspiration of His words
have taken root in form, aligning in me to proclaim
an inspired instruction to the Gentiles.
Jesus is Messiah! The people of Israel rejected Him.

Fr. Larry Gosselin, OFM

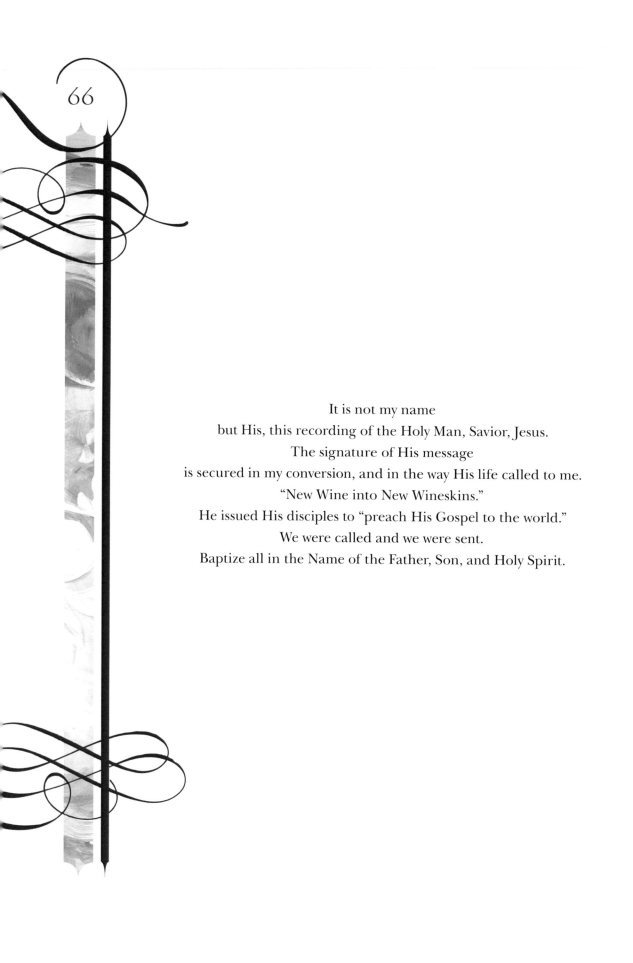

It is not my name
but His, this recording of the Holy Man, Savior, Jesus.
The signature of His message
is secured in my conversion, and in the way His life called to me.
"New Wine into New Wineskins."
He issued His disciples to "preach His Gospel to the world."
We were called and we were sent.
Baptize all in the Name of the Father, Son, and Holy Spirit.

The Publican

It is business as usual
today, in the synagogue.
There the Pharisee in front
is extolling himself in praises.

Behind him sits the sinner,
entreating wrong in humility,
"God be merciful to me, a sinner."
Humiliated by his own sins.

All the humble of the earth
are poured out like a libation.
The Lord hears the cry of the poor;
a prayer of mercy pierces the clouds.

Come, all you, who are lowly
and sincere of heart.
Stand erect before the Lord,
where souls rejoice in mercy,
in the Lord and God of justice,
who sees the heart of the humble.

Fr. Larry Gosselin, OFM

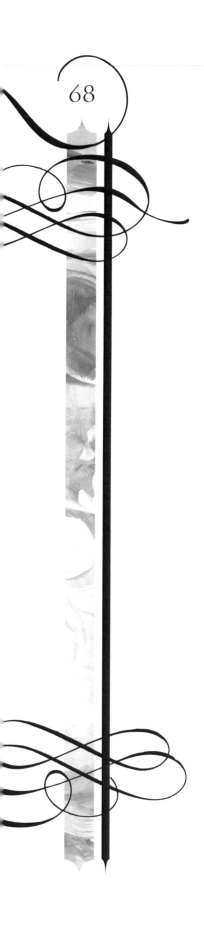

I Heard the Whisper
"You are the Son of God"

Come, listen.
Hear the whisper
heard spoken,
pure of sound, silent
beyond fear.

In the fourth night watch
whispered the voice of love.
"Come, walk to me on water!"
Strong winds buffeted waves
held at bay by the word, "Come!"
The first step, everything, nothing.
Step out, beyond, into the unknown.
Strong, heavy winds rendering a fear.
"Come to me," spoke the One we loved.
Faltering, fearful, I; He reached out to me.
"O, you of little faith, why did you doubt?"
He got into the boat. The wind died down.
We all whispered, "You are the Son of God."
"He walked on water. We must do the same."
Hear the whisper
heard in a storm:
"Come…walk on water."

—Matthew 14:22-33

Who Do You Think You Are?

Just look at you.
Who do you think you are?
You have called yourself a blind man.

You say you see.
So, what did you see?
Is this some joke? Some see-saw?

What did you actually see?
Or rather, who did you see?
You, if blind from birth, cannot say you saw
anything.

I tell you, I saw Him,
"The Man by the Sea of Galilee."

"Let's say you saw
a man who walked by the sea.
But how?
You were born blind at birth!
So how can you see?
Here…are these your parents?
They must know that you were born blind.

"Yes, he is our son.
And we know he was born blind.
How can he see? We don't know…
Why don't you ask him?
For it was he who said he saw.
We do not see, nor can say how this happened.
Ask him yourself…he is of age. He can speak for himself!"
He said he saw
"A Man by the Sea of Galilee."

Fr. Larry Gosselin, OFM

We, your elders, see this as a sin,
to claim he saw a man by the Sea of Galilee…
to say he had no sin and was free, therefore, to see.

So, we say that you could not see
A man by the Sea of Galilee

Just look at you!
Who do you think you are?
You call yourself a blind man.

"How can you tell me
'I did not see the man who set me free?'
Are you the ones who are blind from birth?"

We say that we can see
that you are blind from birth.
How dare you tell us what we need to see!

We do not want to see
this man from the Sea of Galilee.

Such *seeing* is too much!
You need to say that you did not see
a man whom you say spoke to you by the Sea of Galilee.

We are not blind.
We can say that you did not see
this man you say set you free by the Sea of Galilee.

Just look at you!
Who do you think you are?
You who call yourself someone who can see.

"You ask too much
to say that I did not see a man,
One who set me free by the Sea of Galilee."

How can we see?
Show us to him yourself
so that we can say for ourselves, we saw…

This man you say, the one you saw
who set you free by the Sea of Galilee.

Fr. Larry Gosselin, OFM

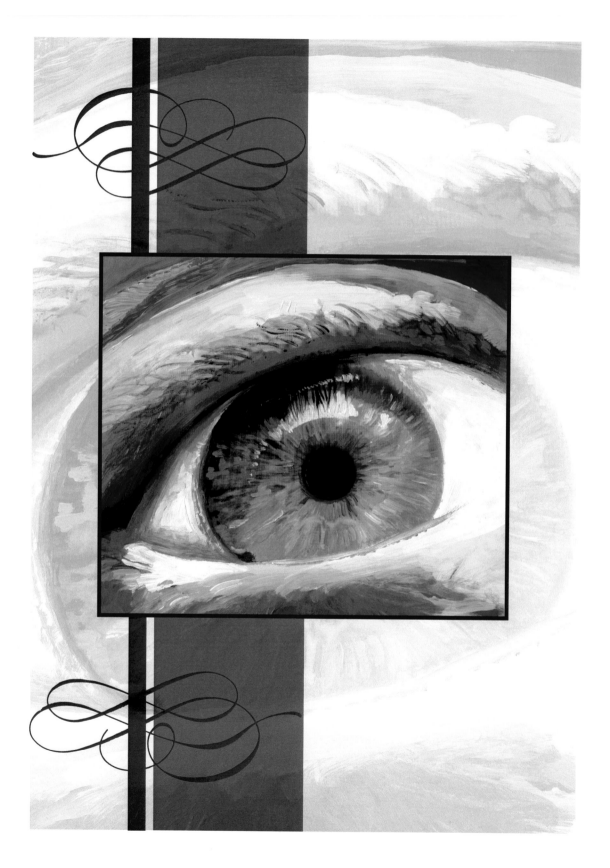

Eye for Eye,
Truth for Truth

Fr. Larry Gosselin, OFM

Eye

for

eye.

I

want

an

eye

for

the

truth.

Hate

demands

a hurt for a hurt.

Hatred as blood, flows.

Love, opens a heart-pouring,

blazing a new forgiven promise.

Enemies turn-around, delivering

goodness to all those they've harmed.

"Be holy, for I, the Lord, your God, am holy."

You have heard it said, and often confirmed

"An eye for an eye, and a tooth for a tooth".

"But what I say, "Is love your enemy?

Do good to those who harm you."

For in this way they will come

to know your Father who

is above, in Heaven.

Seventh Sunday in Ordinary Time
—Matthew 5:36

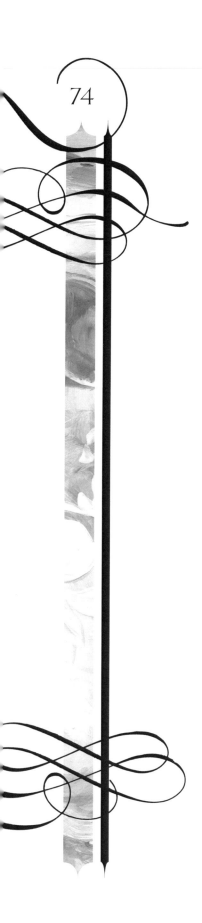

Is there no other way?

You know,
and do not know,
that acting is suffering,
and that suffering is action.
Actor must suffer.
Patient must also act,
within an eternal action,
of having eternal patience.
The way subsists
to give willed consent,
so that the wheel may turn,
but *still*, in patience, forever *still*.
Restless movement…
hearing feet on the street,
vapor arising from dark light,
offering desires that no one wants.
Yet God is hope—
past the soiled rags.
Good Guardian, take charge,
over the cutting edge of my life.

—The Gospel of Mark 8:34-9:1
Inspired from"Murder in the Cathedral" by T.S. Eliot

A Cup of Human Dignity
"The Good Samaritan"

Under a broken tree he lay,
reclining in a heart's agony.
Sorrow filled the scene
painted on the wall of dignity.

As if hidden from eyes
that could recover heart's pain,
forgotten and swept away,
bruised, broken, body like thorn.

Suddenly a soul is wrung
that saw a hidden light glowing.
A sea showering compassion,
told what could be done in love.

Daybreak had come as Christ,
to give a silent kiss upon the heart.
Though broken once, now healed,
enduring the life God gives and asks.

Such love is there to show.
No need for anything but love.
No person can drink wine,
except from a fruitful cup of love.

One is called eternally good,
remembered as the Samaritan of old.
For this one saw not a body,
but a soul residing in the heart of God.

Walking along this road
forged a path to Heaven.

Embracing,

the Christ in one, touched the Christ in another.
The Christ in another, touched the Christ in one.

Fr. Larry Gosselin, OFM

Wellness at the Well

Imagine a well—
this must sound quite curious—
but humor my imaginings for a moment still…
A little tentative world waits to burst forth in you.
A new world opens
there in your soul,
the image of your heart,
like a well flooding forth clear water.

So, you come to the well,
the same old local water source.
A man you never saw before sits at the low stone curb.
He speaks to you about the water,
suggesting…just imagine this…that you could be well,
for you've come to the well not feeling too well.

He asks for a drink of water,
"But our well is too deep," you say.
"And you have no bucket to go down that deeply into it."

He says, "I am flowing water."
Just like that!
"I am that welling deep within you."

You humor Him.
You say, reasonably enough, "But, kind sir, my well is very deep."

"I am wellness in you," He laughs.
"I flow deeply in that thirst you have,
for I am the "Living Water" that your ancestors long desired.

"But, you do not know me well," you say, puzzled.
"My well has been dry for many years," you say.
"And even here, at this well, I come shamefaced."

Suddenly, right there, by the stone retainer,
you feel immediately well; literal wellness
flows naturally inside you, like "Living Water."

He speaks to you about your soul,
right here, on this mountain, pouring out peace
and forgiveness, worthy of worship in spirit and truth.

Worship the Father, the God of Jacob?
You say to yourself, how refreshing and wonderful to hear.

You never before thought of God as "Our" Father.

An old promise comes to you.
It rushes into your heart, springing upwards.

"This man is a prophet," you say to yourself.
"He speaks of our hopes,
and like a mother to her child."
It seems like light leaps into your heart.
You know He brought forth "Living Water" in you.

So, you go to the others.
You tell them, "Come and see this Man,
the One who told me everything that I have ever done."
His loving eyes and words
Will come to you as well, like a fresh breath of life.

And the people drew to draw water from His well.

Fr. Larry Gosselin, OFM

Teaching a Monarch to Fly

Clear skies wide open for freedom of being.
Crispness of morning light sparked new life.
Pure light more than any flame could bring
draws to life a majestic creature of God.
A webbed cocoon breaks clear of water,
like a field of shining sunflowers, comes forth
a monarch butterfly
desiring, striving, spreading new-found wings,
to fly, to fly, to fly free…in what is meant to be.

Who teaches you to spread your wings, to flutter and explore,
to banish obstacles that resist your will to be who you are?
A new world opens; Heaven's sky's the limit, and there you see
no need to remain earthbound, for Heaven-sent you to soar free…

Every way lies open to seek the way above,
for you resurrect, and, neither hunted nor
imprisoned by your liberty, in the flow of love
there "wings" still more revelation in you.
For you are beloved, forgiven,
by your loving, faithful Father.
Renounce shame with the right royal hope of forgiveness.
Rest and fortify yourself in your Father's tender skies.
Feel the sweet balm in your soul: life's purpose.
For you left an offspring and have now returned
Beloved.
Thou Child of the Most High, Glorious God.

Make us one; make us new,
For you are both,
My Beloved.

—Luke 15:11-32

Fr. Larry Gosselin, OFM

79

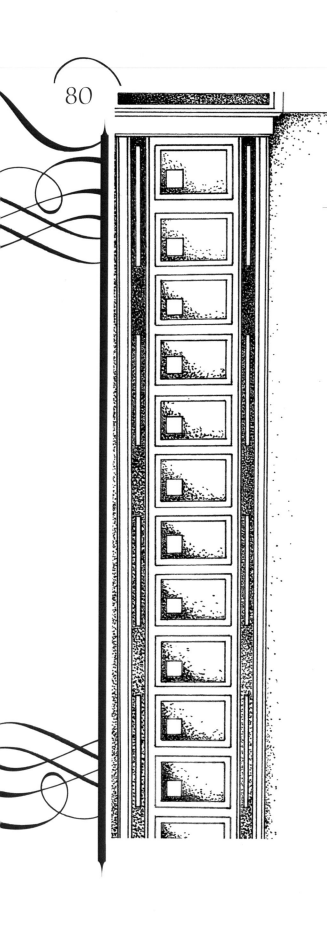

Persistent Mystery

Moses' arms were held up
in a persistent way
that ushered forth
the victory of mystery.

Truly we live under
divine mysteries
too marvelous
for comprehension.

We are permeated by persistent
overshadowing and out-pouring
of divine mystery that floods the soul.

Yet be persistent
in asking,
Where does this all
come from?
And where does this
all lead?

God will surely
secure the rights
of all those who
call out in prayer.

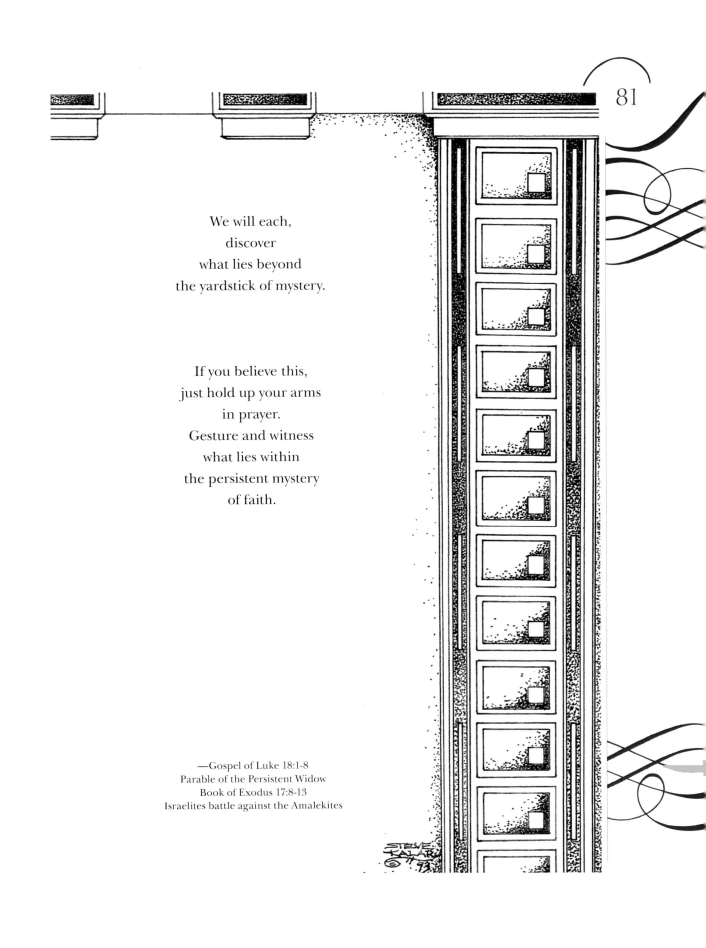

We will each,
discover
what lies beyond
the yardstick of mystery.

If you believe this,
just hold up your arms
in prayer.
Gesture and witness
what lies within
the persistent mystery
of faith.

—Gospel of Luke 18:1-8
Parable of the Persistent Widow
Book of Exodus 17:8-13
Israelites battle against the Amalekites

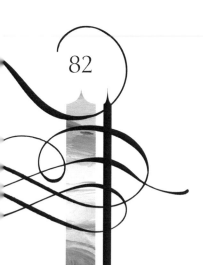

Luciform
from *Luce Formare*

LIGHT

in its own way...

Heavenly light drunk

by eyes seen in earthly ways.

He came for everyone whom He loved

so as to appear to anyone who loved Him:

LIGHT

"My beloved Son,"

shattered with clouds,

"I am well pleased; listen to Him"

came words illuminating Heaven's light,

overshadowing all, heard by those who heard Him:

LIGHT

to take on the form

like the Sun, the Son...the Sun

transforming the darkness into light.

Suddenly in form appeared Moses and Elijah,

who revealed the transfigured One before them:

LIGHT

go down from here;

shine forth from this mountain top

into dark valleys that lie hidden from sight.

"I illume" says He, then declares "Burn on in Me."

"Brighten all, my enlightened ones. Pour My light unto the world."

Second Sunday of Lent
Mathew 17:1-9

A Short Seer Sighted

I can scarcely see
wandering in the crowds,
for I am such a little
one of stature and importance.
I hear someone coming,
this One seems to be calling to me.
I can hear His footsteps and
believing He will offer me forgiveness,
I will climb into this sycamore.
From there I can see His face for myself.
I looked into His face and I saw
a man whose stature spoke as one of pure love.
He said, "Zacchaeus, come down
from the tree, for I wish to dine with you tonight!"
the crowds looked askance at what they
heard, "Zacchaeus, the public sinner, was to have Him?"
But I stood my ground. Yes, I can have Him,
and welcome Him into my home and life, for I seek His love.
He said, "Today salvation has come to this house
because this man, Zacchaeus, too, is a descendent of Abraham."
"For I have come to seek out and to save what has been lost."

—Luke 19:1-10
The Call of Zacchaeus

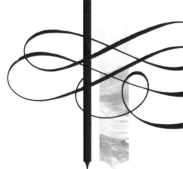

Fr. Larry Gosselin, OFM

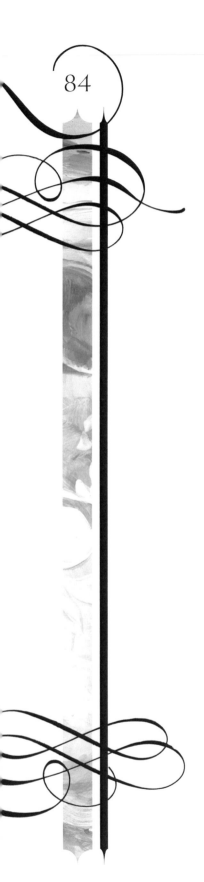

I Know What I Shall Do…

All this talk about winning.

In what ways will the last be first?

All this talk about banks. Who owns what?

More importantly, who owns whom?

And who and what are we indebted to?

Yes, isn't that really the life-long bottom line?

The rain and rumors of floods,

flutter like torn blankets in storm drains,

but really hasn't stopped anything in the streets.

"I know what I shall do…" he said.

I shall settle my accounts with all debtors.

Then, they will surely welcome me into their homes.

The Master looked upon the steward;

even in his dishonesty, he commended him

for prudently acting in the ways of the winning world.

To make friends with dishonest wealth,

is not covered by our eternal insurance plan.

"You will either love one and hate the other," it tells us.

So settle your accounts now.

Who will you trust with your true wealth?

It is really so hard to grasp, this wealth in poverty.

—Gospel of Luke 16:1-13
Story of the Dishonest Prudent Steward

Lazarus and Dives

Father Abraham, do not punish me
for wanton disregard, in these flames of torment,
for my neglect of he, with whom I have been, at the table of plenty.
Look there, at Lazarus stamped on the soul with the seal of bounty,
where the scraps thrown to dogs seem nourishing morsels now to his life.
From where he reclines at your table of blessing,
let him come to me, O, Father Abraham,
make him dip his fingers in cool water
to sooth my scorching tongue.
I ask that you lift him high
beyond this abyss of separation,
that he might rise up to warn others,
of the truth of this land of the dead.
Let him go, that he may tell my five brothers to repent,
lest they too, in their wanton disregard
come to this place of torment.
O, Father Abraham,
if someone were to rise from the dead,
surely they would repent and believe.
But Father Abraham answered:
"If they will not listen to the prophets of old, neither will they listen
even if One were to rise from the dead."
To all it has been proclaimed:
"If you have ears to hear and eyes to see
then heed what you hear, and look so that you might know,
lest that you might believe."
For the One of God, the Son of the Most High,
will come to you and to them in human skin and human need.

—Luke 16:19-31
The Rich Man and Lazarus

Fr. Larry Gosselin, OFM

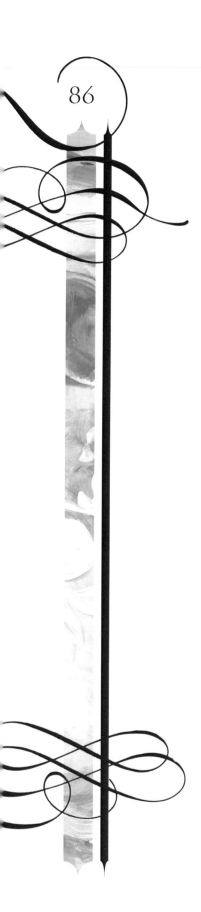

I Must Decrease,
He Must Increase.

Amid water and shore,
deeper than clamorous ocean,
a great light stands still,
shrouded in water and foreground mists,
ripples shimmering about.
There, a world of silence—
soft waves of unshadowed light
speaking now, "Seize my silence!"
"Take hold of my hand!"
The unseen, inward stranger's
light strikes home.
Whose silence are you?
You are not to be less.
Become still more.
All creation watches
the work of God increase.
In winter, a lighted pathway ends,
yet a voice spoke in the wind
saying "You are the "Beloved One", on you
my favor shall ever shine.
For you are unshadowed light!

— Based on John 1:29-34

Sunlight Melts Ice

**"Then I saw another mighty angel
coming down from Heaven,
wrapped in a cloud
with a rainbow
over his head."**
Rev. 10:1
touch ineffable
light and depth
dwelling beyond,
as spring flowers
break through snow,
budding as to know
the light beyond cold.
So as a seeker of light
waits now, as in cold,
growing, knowing
light to be life
from above.
Seeking
light
that
melts
the snow.

Fr. Larry Gosselin, OFM

Seed to the One Who Sows
Bread to the One Who Eats

Yellow seeds on the stonecrops
golden as the late leaves of a cherry tree.
I hold them in front of me as I speak to them.
"Bear rich fruit! Produce the abundant harvest!
Be planted in rich soil. Grow among the thistles!
Be not choked by thorns, scorched by sun,
withered for lack of roots."
Fall upon good soil.
See, Understand, Listen!
Hear the parable of the Sower!
The seed that falls on good ground
bears fruit, a hundred, sixty, thirty-fold.
When a seed has awakened to what really is,
it grows free in a chain, a consequence of growing.
Ah, to be properly planted and ready to produce fruit.
Groan within yourselves as you await this new adoption.
They said to Him, "Why do you speak to them in this way?"
He answered, "So that all may have knowledge of the mystery."
Once again, one is here, and once again, one is learning to grow.
Seemingly nothing is changed, even though everything is changed.
In the morning of the clear autumn, the time of harvest, stand erect.
You are the seed by the One who has sown, bread to the one who eats.

—Parable of the Sower

Fr. Larry Gosselin, OFM

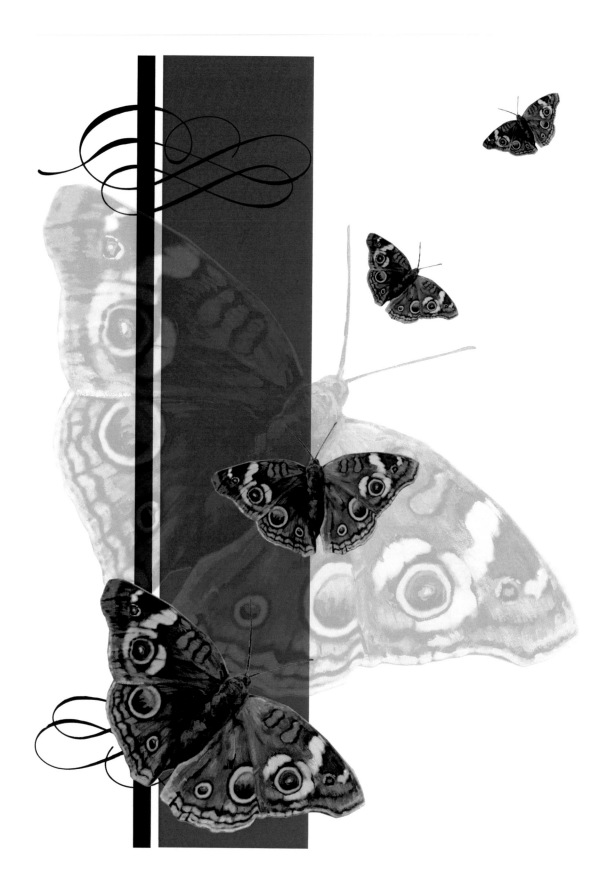

Sometimes I Feel Butterflies Dancing in My Mind

Heavy iron chains,

heavy as they are, especially to lock up,

can seem light, their weight disappearing,

because another chain, made of waves, lands,

winds, smiles, joys, sighs, can bind us in gossamer.

The Master, Yes, the Master gives us freedom from chains.

No muddy, empty, cold or distant ironclad monstrosity can claim us.

This place has clouds, sunshine, freedom coming and going.

Like butterflies dancing in my mind,

our soul has no prison in God,

but as a diamond in the rough,

we are opened to the light

of a new day.

I ask you. Yes, I ask you.

Who do you belong to?

And whose are you?

But love and a life

purchased for you

to be lived out

being set

Free.

St. Paul's Letter to Philemon 9-10; 12-17

Fr. Larry Gosselin, OFM

The Work of God Increase

Story of the Prodigal Son

The work of God increase.
Make clear a way from wayward trends.
In winter light the pathway ends,
As voice of the windward speaks:
"You, Beloved One,
on you my favor rests,
for you are light unshadowed;
You've conquered every test.

Warmth of Morning Rain

Drips in the early morning.
A young boy buried in thought
behind the glass of windowpane.
Streetlight makes the falling rain
patter hard amidst a darkened sky.

Though alone against the drilling rain,
he's clearly wrapped in its embrace,
secure within, protected.

He lives deeply in his heart,
with power to be saved
humbly secure
with life.

Fr. Larry Gosselin, OFM

June's Gloom
Bright Bloom

They do not love that do not show their love.
—Wm. Shakespeare, *Two Gentlemen of Verona*

Cloudbanks
over coastal shores
hidden light
indwelling fog.

Hidden and bidden
shadowed, bedewed.

Light that doesn't reveal itself
is not light.

Love's eternal light
seems sometimes
hidden and still,
yet, here in
the "Stillness of Being",
Love is radiating light.

For June's gloom
promises bright blooms.

To be bright
all must shine
with pure light.

Light will bloom,
to enlighten the gloom.

To be bright as light
Love must show
Love as light.

Climatically, the month of June brings seasonal fog
that blankets the central coastline of California,
hence, locals refer to it as "June Gloom."

Fr. Larry Gosselin, OFM

Just Ask the Wind

Out of a town's history comes the memory of one, El Padre.
Dawn and twilight reveling in the churchy history of this one noble man.
For the people knew, all of them knew, the light of his words and ways.
In him there was One Faith, One Lord and One Community of friends.

He has crossed over the stream, to the place where a new stream flows on.
We, standing on this side of the bank are listening to the sound of the water,
Looking down into the passing current, remembering his reflection.
In the swirls and ripples of time,
both his great words and vision beteem the tide together.

We again begin to collect the iridescence of his mastery.
All rejoice for him that he is free, and that we have been set free through him.
His is to be now as the wind, buried in the thoughts and memories of all.
Just ask the wind. It billows his name, divine master and maker, Fr. Virgil Cordano.

Pray for us
as we remember.

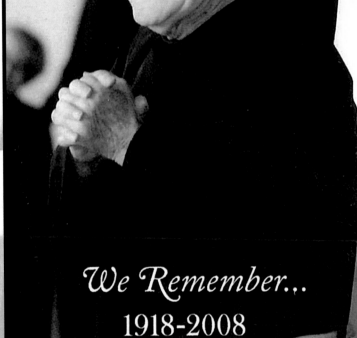

Fr. Virgil Cordano, OFM

We Remember...
1918-2008

Two Insomniacs meet at chapel
(Three O'Clock A.M.)

Suddenly awakened and still dazed,
I bumbled along, sleepy-eyed, down
the long hall of the convento in the Old Mission,
heading for the chapel to take time to be
with the One who also never sleeps.

There, in the dark of night
I stumbled into another
insomniac,
my friend, and former Provincial,
Fr. Louie.
He was heading for the same place.

Spontaneously, and coincidentally, we laughed.
Where are you going at this hour of the morning?
was the mutual question.

So, you're going to pray.
May I join you?
I have nothing better to do,
or in fact,
there is nothing better to do,
at this hour of the morning.

I can't imagine a better place or person
To share my insomnia with than you, dear brother.

To be alone with you,
And with the One
Who never sleeps.

Fr. Larry Gosselin, OFM

La Punta del Dedo de Cristo
(The fingertip of Christ. Tip of the iceberg)

"The body is one,

though many parts.

And so it is with Christ,

many though one, we are in Christ.

Hidden in Christ, we become most useful.

The hands cannot say to the head, "let me be you".

So what part of this grand Body of Christ am I to be?

Pointedly, I motioned and indicated the fingertip:

To be one who points to the One who loves.

I hoped to be the useful index finger:

just the mere tip, only the tip.

To be the tip of the iceberg,

but hidden below it.

A force to be reckoned with,

a presence that peacefully floats above the water's surface, hiding power that lies under.

We rise to the surface with such sheer force when we lie deeply within Christ's shadow.

We are in this Body, to be the very Body of this Christ, and to be formed as one in Him,

we rise to the surface, pointing the way, the way of the pointer, pointing to that above.

We are this Body of Christ. We are the Blood of Christ. Shared and Broken. Poured Out!

Rising to the surface of that which lies hidden within us, we in Him, we are His Body.

Come, become what you were meant to be; eat what you have become. His body lives.

Living in His Body, eating His bread, appoints us; we are the price that has been paid.

He spoke of His Passion, passionately being in us, passing through us, as His Passion.

We are this Body of Christ! We are this Blood of Christ! Shared! Broken! Poured out!

Tears of Forty Years

Some time ago there was a wounding.

From this commenced a live vocation.

I have seen both: the lesion and the lesson.

To believers, no explanations are necessary.

To nonbelievers, explanations seem insufficient.

Yet long ago, in St. Augustine, lived a restless heart,

That fulminated in St. Monica, the tears of forty years:

the restlessness to encounter Christ of our great longing,

the restlessness of the spiritual quest, the restlessness of love.

May we not be anesthetized away from the passion of such longing.

Become restless in your relationship with Our Father, restless for His love.

Her tears of forty years

are like a drop in the bucket

of the joy that she would find.

For Augustine had come to faith;

a heart that did not sleep, but was alive.

Awaken to love God and to be a lead for others.

Oh, my people! Look into your hearts and see,

Open yourself to it, "Let yourself be restless for God."

May Saints Augustine and Monica, mother and her son,

instruct us: Never lose sight in the glory and grace of God.

Lead us to the place of longing where we fulfill our hearts

and become

"Restless until Resting in Thee!"

Inspired by the homily of Pope Francis
For the Feast Day of Sts. Augustine and Monica
Given to the Augustinians' General Chapter.

Fr. Larry Gosselin, OFM

Unshadowed Light

Kelly Green, Lily White

I gave
my friend
a new name.
I call him Lily.
And even though
his name is Kelly,
and he's as green as
the Luck of the Irish,
in an Italian shadow,
"Lily" suits him so well.
I know it's not a name
for a man, but I think it
just fits him well, so well.
I see and think of him as
"The Lily of the Field",
blossoming alive,
shining in light.
He is spring,
life giving,
pure light.
Kelly green
in lily white.
"I am the rose of Sharon,
the lily of the valleys.
His right hand embraces me."

From the Song of Solomon 2:1, 6
In Memory of Brother Kelly Cullen, OFM

This was the last photo taken in Rome, Italy of Br. Kelly Cullen, OFM just hours before he passed from this world,

Fire and Water

"I set before you fire and water."
Sirach 15:15

Two birds,
in one tree:
Birth in water,
Cross of fire.
Good and Evil.
Life and Death.
Set one's course
to be alive: to live.

The blind go their way, as in night,
seeking their way, brushing the darkness,
knowing neither shadow nor light.

Those given sight, go as in the day,
seeing the light, seeking the light of day,
knowing both shadow and light.

Perhaps both saw something blindly:
the blinding darkness or blinding light,
showing both shadow and light.

Yet the course is set:
sky above, earth below.
Stand upright, and discern
the divine waves of eternity.
Look not into the shadows
where true life cannot abide.
Look carefully now into the light:
see before you… fire and water.

Singer and the Singing Cloud

A white cloud floats power down

that arises in the sunlight, like a bird, hovering.

It burns as red rays of light upon the brows below, touching each soul.

A wordless proclamation reverberates in the hearts of all:

"Let go fear; gather all the people as one.

Speak your new languages...proclaim boldly".

The singer sings the clouds.

Today a new birth,

all ordered

freshened,

descending,

orchestrated outpouring of fire

glowing brightly above the heads

and into the hearts of all people,

who bend back, lift their arms, and cry out

Come Consoler,

Come Paraclete,

Come Comforter,

Come Holy Spirit!

So dangerous and profound to behold.

Can there be anything more difficult?

Or anything that is not made new by this outpouring?

In the silence, in the winds that howl

fear will blow asunder,

and you will behold as beheld.

You are one with Me,

By Me,

In Me

C

O

M

E

Fall Afresh!

Fr. Larry Gosselin, OFM

Holy Spirit:
Finest Light

Holy Spirit,
Your light appears
as essence of luminous mystery,
bearing glistening fruit, savoring of your sweetness.
Love
Peace
Charity
Patience
Kindness
Goodness
Gentleness
Endurance
Faithfulness
Self-Control.
Holy Spirit
Your work is one,
your substance delivered to all,
bearing glistening fruit, savoring of your sweetness
in pure abundance, on the wings of a dove.

Unshadowed Light

Holy Spirit:
White Shadow

Holy Spirit
dwells in clear beauty,
cloudless day, starry nights,
"all that is best of dark and bright."
One is mellowed to be that tender light.

Wisdom

To see less of worldly things,
more of God in the living Spirit.

Understanding

To grasp and realize Heaven's truth
while discerning more of the sight of God.

Counsel

To choose what is pleasing to God
with that which proves good for ourselves.

Fortitude

To have strength to bear our own crosses
and overcome the obstacles in our paths.

Knowledge

To know and avoid dangers to our soul;
cherishing gifts of the mind to know God.

Piety

To love God more tenderly and confidently
by doing everything in loving ways for God.

Fear the Lord

To have an attitude of divine reverence, awe,
in all things of God and to despise and avoid evil.

Holy Spirit
bright and light
found by all who seek.

Holy Spirit
I love you. Come to me,
Come into me and breathe
your breath of new life upon me.

Choose Something
Like a Star

Observe a
sweet yoke
in darkness,
when the light
glows only dim.
Vision is blinded.
The dark can be a
womb of your birth.
Let truth see you free!
You, child of light, are
in love,
are loved,
held in love,
as life comes.
Choose something
like a star, in waiting
upon your light into love.
This light is set in the heavens,
where, in love and light, all will see.
Give up all other worlds except the one
to which you belong in the light of heaven.

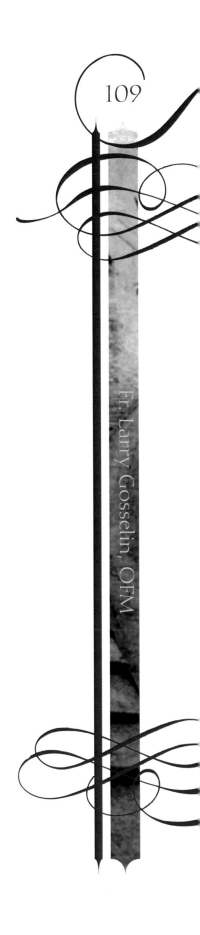

Fr. Larry Gosselin, OFM

a Surprising Radiance

by St. Symeon, the New Theologian

*All of a sudden as I was meditating
…you appeared from on high,
greater, much greater than the sun,
and, from the heavens,
brilliantly you shone down into my heart
…O, what burst of fire!
O, what movements of flame
stirring within me, miserable one
that I am.*

In the Cistern

They brought me to
the Cistern of the Prince,
where deep called upon deep.
This well may give life-saving water,
or empty, shallow, defiling rottenness.
Strange consequences come by remotest causes.
The arrogant passion of a fanatic striving for power
to do the nearly right thing for the clearly wrong reason,
defines the very last temptation, perhaps the greatest treason.
Therefore, this cistern may offer my demise or show best utility.
Now, my good angel, whom God, in grace, appointed as my guardian,
let me no longer suffer at the burnished sword's end, but rise from here.
For through the years, searching in many ways, I find myself a servant of God.
Thus is my new way made clear, for now I see the true meaning made sharp and plain.

Yet, temptation will not end this way,
for grace will rise to a new beginning.
God always gives us reason, and hope.
The manner can take form even in dark air.
So, rise up from this cistern;
for the prophet's call beckons.
Ignite the candle. Torch the flame.
Come in sight of all. Walk in full light.
You have been prophet from the day of birth,
fearlessly pass from deception beyond description.
Retain that lost wonder. Abide in the coming of day.

"Before I formed you in the womb, I knew you;
before you were born, I set you apart,
and appointed you to be a prophet to the nations!"

Based on the Book of the Prophet Jeremiah 38:6

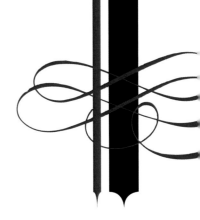

Fr. Larry Gosselin, OFM

The Temptation

In the desert,
stage was set,
pain and glory
facing:
needing,
bleeding,
pleading.
Three contests spoke
from kingdoms
of the world.
In splendor
Came
the choices:
Make bread
from stones!
Throw yourself
down here!
Prostrate and
so worship me!
Secretive, spectacular,
seductive temptations
seeking to transmute.
Jesus stood his ground.
Yes, I change all things,
water to fine wine,
bread to living food,
stone hearts into love.
Christ stood upon the mountain
saw the bottom of his needs and deeds.
Then angels came and ministered to Him.

Fr. Larry Gosselin, OFM

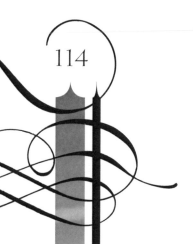

Getting Back to Going Forward

What was the very last thing you noticed,
in thinking back to your hand on the plow?
Did you expect to return to what once was, now?
Has it all already been furrowed following the yoke?
What do you think becomes of the land thus planted?
Do you know the depth of growth and how deep to plow it?

Where have you been for the last three hours?
What has been planted in the past three rows?
What have you seen in the last three miles?
Are you getting to go where you were going?

The past, what has been and done, has been buried.
Now is not the time to look backwards.
Leave the plow and burn the yoke!
Or give it away for food or fodder.
Now, *"Siempre Adelante!"*
Go forward with your
staff and cloak
reborn.
Be planted on good, rich soil.
Plow into new fields of growth!
Take the yoke of promise in hand.
The harvest will come, in the future.
Be stouthearted; look for it in the field.

Based on First Book of Kings 16:21
The call of Elisha by Elijah

Open Field

People, like seeds,
as if in an open field,
spread, set, draw and sprout,
in keeping with each unique life.

Time passes, branches touch,
winds whip; we all hear the birds' song.
Their message renews hope, in love sung.
A tone remembered, a passing word, here and there.

From the field
another voice sounds, echoes,
calm and certain, gathering the living together,
as if by mastered music never orchestrated before.

People hear it repeated
Some rejoice and some rebel.
Yet, we are one in our natural steps to the sound.
You can hear, and you may know the grace of love spoken.

Enter the field.
Lay your cares down upon the fallow ground.
Plant yourselves as if seedlings longing for growth.
Take root in the common soil where all who hunger to thrive are planted.

For it is love
that gives us abundant life.
It is God who gathers us into this field.
It is our shared destiny to discover the fullest growth.

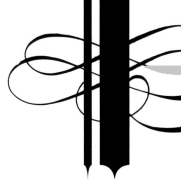

Fr. Larry Gosselin, OFM

Unshadowed Light

Unseen Sun Day

You say, you see.
Yet, if you say, you see,

your blindness remains.

Moving through the dust of years.
Passing through the musth* of fears,
I looked at my soul, not able see it, as it is
faded in a haze of blackened grey mist.

This man came, spitting, put earthen clay
upon my closed eyes. Now I can see again.

I was blind, but now I see,
No longer blind.
I have new sight,
while former dark facades become light.

My eyes as soul-bright windows
opened, born, light, white.

"I can see, I can see, I can see,"
said the man, who all knew was blind.
"Who was this man who opened
my eyes and my soul so that I could see?"

"I am He. You see Him speaking.
No longer will you dwell in darkness.
I came into the world to give sight
to those who cannot see, and blindness
to those who choose not to see."

"Give me sight, O Lord, so that I
may always see
in Your light."

*musth-being in a state of dangerous frenzy

The Dead Man Came Out

I had arrived,
at the last door.
Death.
Prematurely, possibly;
nonetheless permanently.
So I thought.
A giant boulder was placed,
bolting and blocking the tomb.
Death.
It was like a bad smell in the noses
of the good people weeping in Bethany.
So we thought.
Martha, Mary, my beloved friend, Jesus,
came to the tomb after four days, weeping.
Death.
Martha said, "Lord, if you had only been here
our brother would not have been laid in this place."
So they thought.
"Your brother will rise, if you believe. Do you believe?"
"Yes, Lord, I have come to believe that you are the Christ!"
Death…
shall be no more. Your brother will rise. "Lazarus, come out!"
The dead man came out, bound in linens, "Untie him and let him go."
So I thought,
I have been raised from the dead. I live now in this One we call, Jesus.
He has opened the eyes of the blind, and now he has raised me up to live.

Fr. Larry Gosselin, OFM

When I Die

When I die
I want your hands to rest upon my eyes.
I want to feel the light and wheat of your hands.
I want to pass on to you the softness of our changed destiny.

When I die
I want to give you everything that I have.
I want all the love that there is between us to continue.
I want you to possess all that can teach you the song of my love.

When I die
I want you to know the treasure that we are together.
I want to give you the inheritance that I entrust into your hands.
I want to give to you all that I possess for your future keeping treasure.

Therefore,
Being now of full heart and soaring spirit,
I bequeath to you,

Morning light at the break of dawn, may you never forget new quiet light.
Fresh spring rains on flower petals, may you see beauty even in showers.
Full moons on summer nights, may you rest upon memories of lasting joy.

And, finally, my most precious possession:

Love! Love! Love!

Hold these treasures in safekeeping.
May they greatly profit in your heart.

Lent, Like a Little Springtime

Lent, which means, "Little Springtime", begins on Ash Wednesday, in just a few days more. Always it seems, and I mean always, that Lent just sneaks up on us, and catches us off guard. It is a lot like life; real life disrupts unexpectedly, suddenly, so as to begin events anew. After all, Jesus reminds us, life is like the seed that must be disrupted from lying dormant, then taken, buried in the ground, dying to itself, and this is what produces new life. Lent is like that, an interruption from just going on, existing, lying dormant, sleepwalking, to starting over, planting anew, growing through, coming into being a new "you"! Yes, this season brings a major interruption to the "status quo".

Compared to Winter, a time in many places where "the snow flies", a season of quiet, slumber, rest, dormancy, something is just waiting to break forth, lying in wait. And then comes Springtime, with its sudden burst of welcomed warmth and forgotten, unexpected light. This just awakens everything, calling it to come back, to wake up, get up, it is time for the season of light to bloom. For bloom we must, or we shall die. Yes, life and death are held close to each other at this first burst of Springtime. For we human beings as well, it is a time to begin the special season of Lent, remembering, "You are from the dust; ashes to ashes. Resist the allurements that come from darkness. Turn from sin, which causes death and seek new life. The light is shining for all to see."

Lent is a time to be cherished; it is a time to cherish. Cherish this special time allotted for us just to grow. Often I hear people say, "I just can't wait for Lent. I just need it and I want it." What a beautiful anticipation that is, to have someone's longing and realization of what they need.

They need and want to take time to grow spiritually, not only to strive for growth, but to thrive in living in this new way. They need to quiet the urgings of the flesh and the world, to seek a deeper meaning and calling in life, to listen, to pray, to reach out to others who are in need, to seek a conversion of the heart, and to follow, follow, follow Jesus Christ more intimately on His journey of life, entering His passion, carrying His cross, embracing His death and then entering into His resurrection and new life.

As we ponder this opportunity of appreciating the mystery of new life that is given to us in Christ, let us take this moment to set forth a "place and plan of penitent practice". And let's think of this as the four P's.

Lightness of Lent

Forty days more,
then Easter.
Life buds forth
new risen!

But now we stop,
turn, learn.
The season tells us
begin again.

Like springtime
is Lent;
our spirit longs
to be renewed.

Strange how it
strikes you—
peculiar, special
new light.

Lightness
of old, given
purple crown
a king.

Light kindles
memory—
Follow the call,
"Come, see!"

May we gesture
with ashes—
Remember: you are
unto dust…

given to Light.

Fr. Larry Gosselin, OFM

Whisper of Easter

Imagine a world…
I know…this sounds as if imposture,
but just follow foreshadowing
for a brief while…

Cupped in your hand lies a piece of bread.
It is warm and tender, smelling as fresh
as if newly drawn from the oven.
It conjures up a delicious
desire, a palate to eat
to share with others.
Set in your
hand is
life.

You are this:
The Bread of Life.
Adumbrating bread*,
Foreshadow of banquet.
See the foreshadowing.
Take, eat this, all of you.
Bread shared for many.
You hold in hand, Life.
The Bread of Life.
You are this.

Jesus,
Bread of Life,
given to many,
to be, to share, to eat.
Feed us with food of life.
You are our foreshadowing,
holding us in the palm of your hand,
we hold You in the palm of our hands, to be
for others what You are for us: to be bread, shared.
Cupped in your hand lies a piece of bread, the whisper of Easter.

*Adumbrating: to have a shadow forward;
to foreshadow vaguely, to intimate, to symbolize.

A Palm Between Two Branches
Palm (Passion) Sunday

The woven
palms
of tree
branches
came of wind,
rain,
night
and tomorrow…
the rapture
of triumph,
and the sudden death.
Jesus, bound into triumphal glory,
set free to soar deep
into Heaven's abyss.
O, city of future promises O, wretched Jerusalem!
Did you stand smugly before these gates of triumph?
Were you there within sight of the gruesome Cross?
Did you fall in rapture at the open void of the dark tomb?
Are you here now, today, in the journey of God's glory?
Do you have hands full of palm fronds woven of painful joy?
"Say to
the daughter
of Zion, Behold
your King comes
now meek and riding
upon a colt, a foal of
a beast of burden.
"Hosanna,
the King of David!
Behold your King on high!
Blessed is he
who comes in the name
of the Lord.
And the people ask,
"Who is this King?"

May You be Eastered in Christ

You have been Eastered in Christ, into Life.

This wonderful gift promises renewal.
Those aware of its proclamation,
hear it sounded inside their hearts.
It speaks the wordless secret of ultimate joy.

In the church silence, the priest blesses water.
How beautiful is water, how humble and selfless.
Christ has made water miraculous with His life.

Water is our birth.
As a quiet pond reflects light
so, simplicity mirrors in clear water.
May we be mirrored anew in Christ.

Jesus said to the storm, "Be Still!"
And it was.
Jesus calms busy minds, restless spirits.
Jesus comforts us in stillness.
Jesus said, "I am the living water."
And so we come, we come to the water.

Come to this water, often.
Receive a candle.
How beautiful you appear in its light.
For you are beautiful in the light of Christ.
Joy, marvelous joy, overcomes our hearts today.
It cannot be contained!

Alleluia! Alleluia! Alleluia!
We can be no longer silent.
Yet, there is no other word to speak but...
Alleluia! Alleluia! Alleluia!
May you be Eastered in Christ!

Fr. Larry Gosselin, OFM

Unshadowed Light

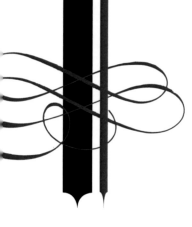

Where is this Place, Easter?

All life
leads us
to a place that we call Easter!
We come into the sweet yoke of love
that invites us all to be in her warm embrace.
Her smile sparkles again to win our hearts from pain.

To sit, to sigh, to weep, to faint, to die
but no…to live.

New life!
Jesus
is Risen!
Alleluia!
The light of His day has dawned.
Wounds sealed, life revealed, lives healed!
Christ dawns new, beyond the secrets of the grave.
His light shines crowning away winters of life's woes.

To see, to hear, to touch, to kiss, to live.

He Lives
Here
in our hearts
in the place we call Easter.
Standing, we pray, bestowing water of bliss
fire, smoke into the night sky for the light of life.
May the dawn of new light break the chains of darkness.

To celebrate, to savor, to believe, to trust, to love!

In me,
in you, in all of us.

Second Look
on the Second Sunday of Easter

Reflected like a book,
like being hidden in a nook.
it took a second…
Look!

Cross furrows deeply imbedded,
as if tattooed upon His forehead,
gave one serious consideration
that he had certainly walked his talk.
He said boldly, "Sin has been behooven,
But all shall be well, all manner of things,
shall be well."
The faces, places He had seen and walked
took me by surprise, wonder, astonishment.
He took my second look, to see He was for real.
In seeing Him, transfigured I became, beholding
what had resembled death, transformed, refulgent life.
"Place your hand in My wounds. See. Believe!"
Blessed are those who have not had a second look,
for they have seen that an end is only the beginning.
Now, believe, here, now, always know and see that
All is well, and all manner of things shall be well; all shall be well.

Sunzrae

Leaping
into the air,
dancing sparkles
of light dazzling white,
upon the water, blue, clear.
Oh, bright is the day of sunzrae.
A small boat flounders in deep water,
coming next is its own heave and grace.
The soul is only a window to let in the light,
the current draws the boat into light's mystery.

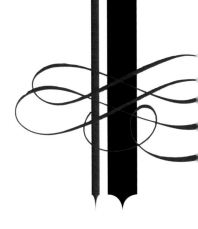

Fr. Larry Gosselin, OFM

But, You gave us your Word

You gave Your Word
that whoever loves You
will keep Your Word.
We know only one Word
and You are the Word
that we continue to feel,
for without Your Word
the Word lives in the shadow of speech,
only attached to glimmerings of truth.

But the air is filled with singing, still.
By singing your Word, You hold us quiet in our hearts, clear of eye
so as to see and hear the promise that speaks ever silently.
In our living abandonment, we are held steadfast to the way of Your Word.
The Word continues to speak clearly from an ancient faith made forever new.
In this silence, the Word says, "I will love you to the end of time."
And where leads this end that cannot die? Has it a season, time, day, moment?
Your love has no limit, no end of eras, just so far as the end of love itself.
The Word speaks not merely in time or space, but in the inward dwelling love.
You gave Your Word to love, and we from our distance will be free from want or fear.
Your Word looms love in us, near and from afar.
I will love you to the very end of love, which is joy.
Hear my Word; I give it gladly.
"The world will no longer see Me, but you will see Me."
A symphony in silence speaks in the stillness of our hearts.

My Word descends upon you.
Holy, Holy, Holy is the Sacrament of My Word.

The Lover and the Beloved

"You seduced me, O Lord,
And I let myself be seduced"

Jeremiah 20:7 (a)

Where do you come from?

"Love."

To whom do you belong?

"Love."

Who gave birth to you?

"Love."

Where were you going?

"Love."

Who brought you up?

"Love."

What is your name?

"Love"

Where do you live?

"Love."

How do you live?

"Love."

"Are you anything except love?"

"Yes!"

"I am my faults, and I have sins."

So then,

"Is there pardon in your beloved?"

"Yes!"

"My beloved is mercy and justice."

Therefore,

"I'm lodged between fear and hope."

Based on the writings of
Blessed Ramon Lull, T.O.S.F.
1232-1315 A.D.
Franciscan Tertiary
"Fool of Love"
The Book of the Lover and the Beloved

Fr. Larry Gosselin, OFM

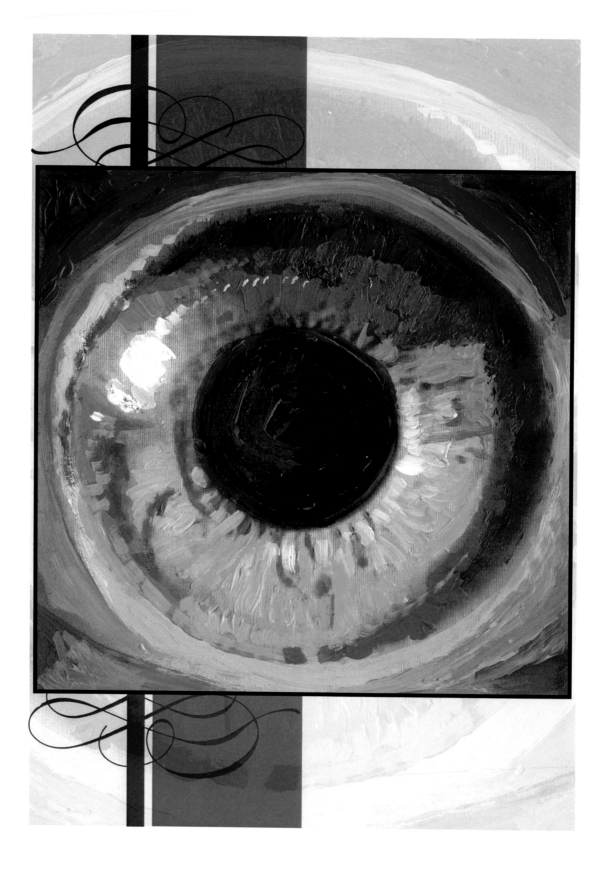

If My Eyes Could See

If my eyes could see
just beyond the sea of people
along the beach of Copacabana,
there in view of "Cristo Redento",
standing in majestic splendor
over the "Marvelous City"
"Cidade Maravilhosa"
Copacabana
by the sea
I'd see
sunlight
even in rain
shine forth from the
One who opened our hearts,
to shine on all with a new light.
Let us then delay no longer, but hasten,
ask, receive, knock and it will be opened.
The one who asks, receives, who knocks is let in.
The Redeeming Christ calls us again on the seashore;
leave your boats, abandon your nets, come and follow me.
Trust in the One who comes to give what is good to the children.
So ask, and more will be given of the Holy Spirit to those who seek.
Our Father, who art in Heaven, hallowed be thy Name. Thy Kingdom come,
Thy will be done on earth as it is in heaven. Give us this day our daily bread,
and forgive us our trespasses, as we forgive those who trespass against us, and lead
us not into temptation, but deliver us from evil.
Amen.

Fr. Larry Gosselin, OFM

Conclusion

The creative spirit comes from within, the God-within, that Mystery who calls us to be more than we are, calls us to be…

Therefore, my work is an attempt to find the divine spark implanted in me and in each of us, to let it burn a little more brightly by trying new ways of expressing the divinity we all share, that which was part of the "image and likeness" gifted to us at our birthing song.

I wish you His peace, love and mercy, always.

—Fr. Larry Gosselin, OFM

Final Prayer

The Path

Open the door.
Lead me anywhere.
Snow, rain, wind or shine,
Lead me
Take me – lead me
Take me down the path.

Hannah Dillon, 2014
9 years old

Fr. Larry Gosselin, OFM

Biographies

Author: Fr. Larry Gosselin, OFM

Fr. Larry Gosselin, OFM is a Franciscan Friar of the Province of Saint Barbara, a native of Washington State, but a friar of the world. He is presently serving in parochial ministry at Old Mission Santa Barbara, CA.

Fr. Larry, for thirty-nine years of Franciscan life, has lived in a variety of cultural and economic milieus. As minister, he has experienced Christ, on the streets with the homeless in Seattle, on Indian reservations of the Southwest, among indigenous people of Mexico, alongside of the poor in India, and parochial ministry in varied settings. In all places, he has come to know "home" among the People of God. Love for life's adventures and faith has taken him to distant shores and high peaks, humble pueblos and stately provinces, altaplanos plateaus and fertile valleys. Through the peoples and places; time, travel, work, ministry, love, passion, and hard won victories, he has been brought to the place called "poetry."

Poetry, as the place able to contain intimations of a deeper and wider appreciation of the sacred.

Illustrator: Steve Kalar

An artist/aesthetics designer, Steve Kalar was born in Paso Robles, attended Lillian Larson Elementary School in San Miguel and graduated from Paso Robles High School (class of 1970) for which he is a member of the school's Academic Hall of Fame. His adventure in Italy began in August of 1972. Mr. Kalar's parents, Bob and Fern Kalar, offered him the opportunity to study at the California International Programs in Firenze, Italia, where he also attended the Accedemia delle Belle Arti. There he refined his talent in fine arts studio painting and fresco and restoration techniques. According to Steve, "I remember the first morning I ventured into the central market of Borgo San Lorenzo...its beauty of space, seasonal color and daily life have inspired and overwhelmed me for the past 41 years". He lived there off and on for approximately 8 years during the 1970's and early 80's. In the past 35 years he has worked as an artist/aesthetics designer throughout the United States, creating ambiance, special effects, and commissioned artwork for numerous high end projects and clientele.

Editor: Miki Landseadel

Miki Landseadel-Sanders (M.A. in English from CSU Sacramento) has been a secondary teacher for the past 24 years. She and her husband, Mike, own *The San Miguel Mercantile* in San Miguel, California and, in their spare time, grow organic fruit and vegetables on their acre near the town. Miki cantors at Mission San Miguel and participates in variety of church and civic programs in her community. She is the mother of two sons, Aaron and Nick, and grandmother to Miles, Hailey and Owen.

Photographer: Mary Kay Fry

Mary Kay Fry was raised in Idaho and Nevada. Her mother and father loved to travel so she, her brother, and two sisters were fortunate to see many places in the world. In the 1960's memorable trips were taken in a Greyhound bus her father converted into a beautiful, self-contained home. Shipped to Africa, this home on wheels carried the family through Kenya, Uganda, Tanzania, the countries then known as Northern and Southern Rhodesia, and South Africa. Another family adventure in the coach was a cross-continent journey from Amsterdam to New Delhi, India. Mary Kay and her husband traveled part of the way, leaving her parents and sister in Greece for her husband to return to school in California. These experiences created an abundance of visual memories and an awareness of the gift of documenting the world's diverse beauty on film.

The first time Mary Kay visited Assisi, Italy, she felt the profound sweetness of this medieval town that remains much the same as it was when St. Clare and St. Francis lived there 800 years before. A sense of peace permeated the air and bounced off the stone buildings. Wanting to capture what she was feeling, she took photographs of moments that caught her eye and her heart. Rather than words, her photographs became her Assisi journal. She has returned to Assisi ten times over the past thirty years and always looks forward to her next Assisi pilgrimage. Her website is www.peaceprints.com. Mary Kay now lives in Santa Barbara, California.

SECRETARIAT OF STATE

FIRST SECTION · GENERAL AFFAIRS

From the Vatican

His Holiness Pope Francis was pleased to receive the kind gift sent for his acceptance. He appreciates the devoted sentiments which prompted this thoughtful presentation.

The Holy Father gives the assurance of a remembrance in his prayers and sends his blessing.

Peter B. Wells

Monsignor Peter B. Wells
Assessor